DECODING EGYPTIAN HIEROGLYPHS

DECODING EGYPTIAN HIEROGLYPHS

how to read the secret language of the pharaohs

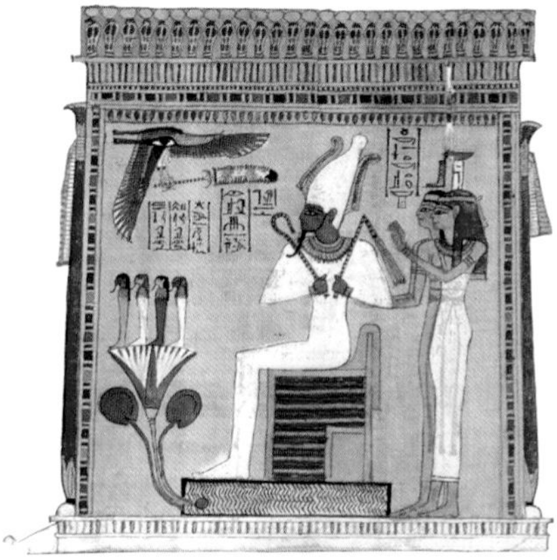

BRIDGET McDERMOTT

Foreword by
JOANN FLETCHER, Ph.D.

CHRONICLE BOOKS
SAN FRANCISCO

CONTENTS

Decoding Egyptian Hieroglyphs by Bridget McDermott

First published in the United States in 2001 by Chronicle Books LLC.
Conceived, created and designed by Duncan Baird Publishers.

Library of Congress Cataloging-in-Publication Data available.

ISBN: 0-8118-3225-2

Senior Editor: Charles Phillips
Designer: Suzanne Tuhrim
Picture Research: Cee Weston-Baker
Editors: Joanne Clay, Karen Frazer
Editorial Assistants: Kelly Bishop, Jessica Hughes, Louise Nixon
Design Assistant: Allan Sommerville
Commissioned maps: Neil Gower
Decorative borders: Sally Taylor
Hieroglyphs set by Nigel Strudwick using fonts created by Cleo Huggins
Typeset in Filosofia; Printed in Hong Kong

Distributed in Canada by
Raincoast Books
9050 Shaughnessy Street
Vancouver, B.C. V6P 6E5

10 9 8 7 6 5 4 3 2 1

Chronicle Books LLC
85 Second Street
San Francisco, CA 94105
www.chroniclebooks.com

NOTE
The abbreviations BCE and CE have been used throughout this book:
BCE Before the Common Era (the equivalent of BC);
CE Common Era (the equivalent of AD).

FOREWORD

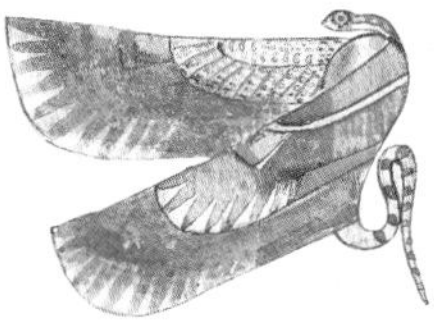

A detail from the sarcophagus image opposite shows a winged cobra, which combines the attributes of Wadjet, cobra goddess of Lower Egypt, and her sister Nekhbet, vulture goddess of Upper Egypt. The pair were often depicted as protectors of the king.

Hieroglyphs contain within them the very essence of ancient Egypt. It was only with their translation in 1822 (see page 11) that the wonders of this historically remote civilization were opened up to us, and since that date generations of scholars have dedicated themselves to studying the tantalizing, complex language first written by scribes more than 5,000 years ago. A grounding in hieroglyphs can help us decipher for ourselves what the ancient Egyptians had to say. Hieroglyphs may be most familiar as the means of recording the pharaohs' achievements, yet they actually contain a range of observations, emotions – and even humour! Nothing can compare to the sense of achievement derived from recognizing and translating one's first word in hieroglyphs.

Decoding Egyptian Hieroglyphs puts hieroglyphic writing in the context in which it appeared. As students, both Bridget McDermott and I struggled with outdated translation methods, lacking books that allowed us to read inscriptions directly from the temples or tombs they embellished – as an integral part of the surface they adorned. Interacting with the scenes they accompanied, the hieroglyphic words and the pictures were meant to be read and understood as a whole. *Decoding Egyptian Hieroglyphs* provides you with the means to enter the world of ancient Egypt, armed with the preliminary knowledge that will enable you to begin to decode the hieroglyphs and eventually pass through into a lifetime of understanding and appreciation. It is therefore with the greatest pleasure that I recommend this book, which is accessible, comprehensively illustrated and crossreferenced – and above all highly readable.

DR JOANN FLETCHER

TIMELINE: EGYPTIAN HISTORY AND THE DEVELOPMENT OF HIEROGLYPHS

Egyptologists are not certain about the exact dating of events before c.664BCE. The dates given here are based on the latest theories. Dynasty 22 ran concurrently with the rival Dynasties 23 and 24.

Early Dynastic Period 3000–2625BCE	Old Kingdom 2625–2130BCE	First Intermediate Period 2130–1980BCE	Middle Kingdom 1980–1630BCE
1st, 2nd and 3rd Dynasties	4th, 5th, 6th, 7th and 8th Dynasties	9th, 10th and 11th (before reunification of Egypt) Dynasties	11th (after unification of Egypt), 12th, 13th and 14th Dynasties
Archaic Egyptian	Old Egyptian →		
		Middle Egyptian	

Wearing a panther skin, the deceased (right) offers the papyrus and lotus – symbols of the two kingdoms of Upper and Lower Egypt – to Osiris, god of the underworld. Osiris holds the crook and flail, emblems of divine kingship. The image is from the sarcophagus of Ankhefenkhonsu, dated to the Twenty-Second Dynasty (945–712BCE).

Second Intermediate Period 1630–1539/23BCE	New Kingdom 1539–1075BCE	Third Intermediate Period 1075–656BCE	Late Period 664–332BCE	Greco-Roman Period 332BCE–CE395
15th, 16th and 17th Dynasties	18th, 19th and 20th Dynasties	21st, 22nd, 23rd, 24th and 25th Dynasties	25th, 26th, 27th (1st Persian), 28th, 29th, 30th and 2nd Persian Dynasties	Macedonian Kings, Ptolemaic Dynasty, Roman Emperors

Traditional Middle Egyptian →

Late Egyptian →

Demotic →

Coptic →

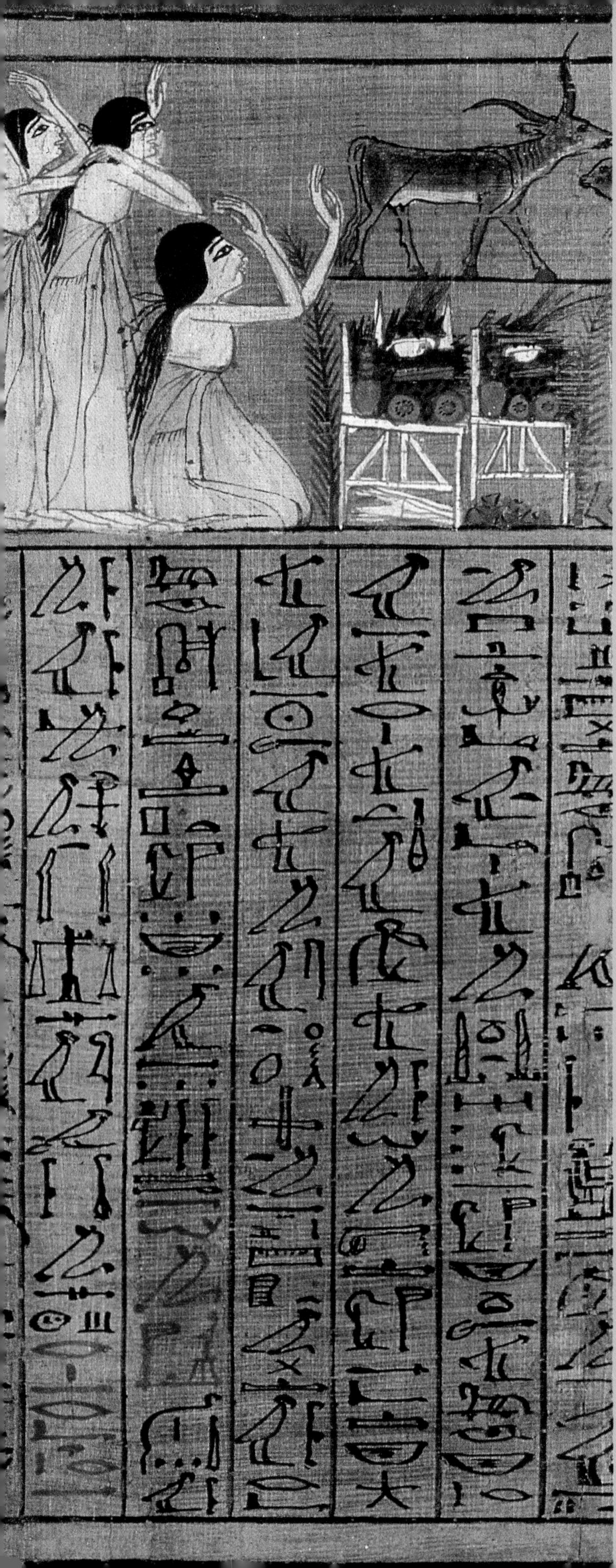

CHAPTER ONE

FIRST STEPS

For almost 1,500 years, hieroglyphs were seen as beautifully depicted but mysterious figures. This chapter takes the first steps on the journey toward an appreciation of this rich treasury of signs, beginning where Egyptologists began their own process of discovery – by tracing the evolution of the language and establishing a view of its basic structure.

Hieratic on a papyrus from the tomb of the scribe Ani (c.1290BCE) contains spell 1 from the Book of the Dead. At top, Ani's goods are carried to his tomb.

DISCOVERY & DECIPHERMENT

In 1799 a French officer at Fort Julien in el-Rashîd in Egypt uncovered a granitic rock carved with three scripts: hieroglyphs, demotic or popular Egyptian, and ancient Greek. The slab was the key to deciphering hieroglyphs.

THE ROSETTA STONE

The officer was a member of a French expeditionary force to Egypt, and copies of the inscription on the slab – later called the Rosetta Stone after European versions of el-Rashîd – were sent to Paris. By examining the Greek text on the slab, scholars saw that the carving commemorated the coronation of Ptolemy V and had been commissioned by priests of Memphis in 196BCE. But it was years before the fourteen lines of Egyptian hieroglyphs were deciphered.

Jean-François Champollion, a precocious French linguist, obtained a copy of the Rosetta Stone inscription in 1808 when he was only eighteen. Fluent in ancient Greek, he compared the hieroglyphs in oval enclosures – which were believed to contain royal names – to the royal names listed in the Greek section of the inscription. Other scholars had identified Ptolemy in Greek and Egyptian. Champollion assumed that the name should be read alphabetically and that each hieroglyph represented a separate letter, and by reading from right to left established the name p-t-o-l-m-y-s. He was able to draw up a small alphabet.

When he saw a copy of an inscription containing the name Cleopatra, he made a longer sign list that enabled him to read names on other monuments. He realized that hieroglyphs used signs that represented both sounds and ideas and he examined the grammar of the language, making his findings public in 1822.

The Rosetta Stone, inscribed with fourteen lines of hieroglyphs, thirty-two lines of demotic Egyptian and fifty-four lines of ancient Greek, is 3ft 9in (1.1m) high and 2ft 4in (72cm) wide. In the hieroglyphic text, one cartouche or oval enclosure containing Ptolemy's name is repeated six times with small changes. Scholars called the enclosures "cartouches" from the French for the paper rolls or cartridges used to hold the powder for muskets, since the enclosures resembled these rolls,

THE LONGEST OF THE PTOLEMY CARTOUCHES READS "PTOLEMY, EVER-LIVING, BELOVED OF PTAH".

THE SHORTEST OF THE CARTOUCHES ON THE STONE CONTAINS SIMPLY THE ROYAL NAME PTOLEMY.

THE HISTORY OF THE LANGUAGE

The four scripts of ancient Egyptian – hieroglyphs, hieratic, demotic and Coptic – can be compared in the artwork opposite. The first and third columns are in hieroglyphic script with a translation in hieratic alongside each. In the right-hand section the top text is a reproduction of a wine recipe dating from 145CE in demotic, while beneath are two fragments of Coptic written in Greek characters except for the two blue letters which are survivals from demotic (see main text).

Around 3000BCE developments in trade brought about crosscultural relationships between Egypt, Mesopotamia and neighbouring countries. The Sumerians of Mesopotamia had developed a system of writing that used pictograms or picture signs and for many years scholars believed that this system was the basis of Egyptian writing. Recent excavations at Abydos, however, have revealed that Egypt had used a pictorial language several hundred years before Mesopotamia.

The oldest surviving examples of written Egyptian date from *c*.3250BCE. At first the pictorial script was used primarily to record royal possessions but by the Old Kingdom (2625–2130BCE) the script appeared mainly in religious or commemorative inscriptions on palaces, temples and tombs, on statues, coffins and sarcophagi and on amulets and jewelry. For this reason the Greeks who ruled Egypt after the death of Alexander the Great in 323BCE called the writing "hieroglyphics" from the Greek words *hieros* (meaning "sacred") and *gluphe* ("carving"). Hieroglyphic writing was in use for more than 3,000 years from the fourth millennium BCE to the fourth century of the Christian era, when – in a Roman-dominated Egypt – it faded into obscurity. The latest known inscriptions in hieroglyphs date from 24 August 394CE and were discovered on the island of Philae in the River Nile in southern Egypt, where a temple to the goddess Isis was still in use in the sixth century CE.

Hieroglyphic signs were written in columns and rows and read from right to left, from left to right or from top to bottom – but never from bottom to top (see page 19). A simplified form of hieroglyphic writing probably first appeared shortly after the introduction of the original hieroglyphs. In the Old Kingdom this simplified form was used for secular administrative papyri as well as for temple accounts and religious texts. In the Greco-Roman period (332BCE–CE395), however, it was used only by priests and in religious contexts – the Greeks named it "hieratic", from *hieratikos* ("priestly"). Scribes wrote hieratic in columns and rows; in rows it read from right to left.

A more rapid form of writing – best described as a shorthand used for administrative documents – first appeared in 724–712BCE and continued in use until the late Roman period (fourth century CE). The Egyptians identified it by a phrase meaning "writing of documents", but it is widely known as "demotic" from the Greek *demotikos* ("popular"), because it was used in secular writing.

A fourth form of written Egyptian was Coptic. This was written in the Greek alphabet but retained seven characters from the ancient Egyptian language. While earlier forms of Egyptian used only consonants in their alphabets (see pages 22–23), Coptic used vowels as well and has helped scholars reconstruct the vowel sounds of hieroglyphic writing. The earliest Coptic texts, which date from the first and second centuries CE, were Egyptian magical writings. The name comes from the Greek *Aiguptia*, "Egypt". After the Arab conquest of Egypt in 640–642CE, Arabic largely replaced Coptic in Egypt.

The language of Egypt is divided by historians into Old, Middle and Late Egyptian. Old Egyptian is dated to 3180–2240BCE and was used in official, funerary and biographical inscriptions. Middle Egyptian (2240–1990BCE) was developed in literary compositions of the Middle Kingdom and continued in use well into the Eighteenth Dynasty (1539–1292BCE). Because it is grammatically consistent, Middle Egyptian is the best place to start when learning to read hieroglyphs. Late Egyptian, dating to 1573–715BCE, is found in official documents, inscriptions and letters.

THE SCRIBAL LEGACY

In ancient Egypt, those able to read or write the elaborate hieroglyphic script were held in great esteem, and often became prominent figures in the religious, military or political realms. Literacy was limited to members of the élite. Highly trained scribes used hieroglyphs to facilitate the administration of the state and to document political and religious events.

The scribe Nebmerutef sits at work before Thoth, the god of writing and knowledge believed by ancient Egyptians to have revealed the divine secrets of hieroglyphic writing. This alabaster piece was carved c.1350BCE during the Eighteenth Dynasty (1539–1292BCE).

THE ROLE OF THE SCRIBE

From the age of seven, boys from Egypt's upper classes attended school at temple, where they practised their writing on *ostraca* (fragments of pottery or limestone) or on wooden writing boards that were coated with gypsum. Pupils probably also learned words and phrases by heart by chanting them. Boys are also known to have studied literary compositions including stories and wisdom texts.

It is thought that Egyptian further education began between the ages of thirteen and fifteen, when students were expected to embark on an apprenticeship. Among the many trades open to educated young men, the military and scribal professions were particularly highly regarded. Those who chose to become scribes enjoyed promising prospects – qualified scribes could expect to graduate to prestigious administrative positions in a range of sectors. Military scribes were responsible for recruiting and organizing the army and its supplies. Some scribes acted as architects, while others designed the plans for decorating royal tombs and temples with hieroglyphs and pictures, and supervised the artists and craftsmen who carried the plans out.

Individual scribes, even if they came from relatively humble backgrounds, were sometimes promoted to positions of high office. Imhotep, the scribe and architect of the step pyramid at Saqqara, was even worshipped as a god after his death, as was another famous scribe, Amenhotep son of Hapu (see page 17).

The ancient Egyptians revered literacy, and even élite men who were not scribes sometimes commissioned statues of themselves kneeling crosslegged on the ground in the pose that characterized the profession. The scribe is usually depicted with rolls of writing material stretched across his knees. The Egyptians wrote on bone, clay, ivory, linen, metal and vellum, but *ostraca* and papyrus were more widely used. Scribes selected small rectangular sections or rolls of papyrus, which were several metres in length. Egyptian books, in the form of scrolls, were usually stored in boxes or jars.

The hieroglyphic word for "scribe" *sš/sesh* (see pages 20–23 for transliteration and pronunciation of hieroglyphs) starts with an image of the scribal palette and tools; the determinative sign (see page 24) is a kneeling male figure that represents a scribe at work. The scribal palette consisted of black and red inks that were used to distinguish between sections of text. The black pigment was derived from carbon, while the red was extracted from two types of iron oxide and ochre. Both pigments were moulded into small cakes which were mixed with gum and water. Pens and brushes were crafted from the firm, straight stems of reeds or from slivers of wood which were bruised at one end until the fibres separated and formed bristles. The word "to write" *sš/sesh* is almost identical to the word for "scribe", and was pronounced in the same way. It shows the scribal palette and pen followed by the image of a sealed papyrus roll.

A PRIVILEGED PROFESSION

These extracts from a Middle Kingdom (1980–1630BCE) literary composition, *Satire of the Trades*, expound the advantages of joining the scribal profession:

"I have seen many beatings ...
Set your heart on books!
I watched those seized for labour –
There's nothing better than books!
It's like a boat on water.
Read the end of the Kemit Book,
You'll find this saying there:
'A scribe at whatever post in town,
He will not suffer in it;
As he fills another's need,
He will not lack rewards'.

"They gave themselves the scroll as lector-priest,
The writing-board as loving son.
Instructions are their tombs,
The reed pen is their child,
The stone surface their wife.
People great and small
Are given them as children,
For the scribe, he is their leader."

The scribe Amenhotep son of Hapu, here portrayed as an old man seated in the scribal pose, served under pharaoh Amenhotep III (1390–1353BCE) and supervised the most extensive building program known in ancient Egypt. This black-granite statue is from the Karnak temple; its inscription tells of the scribe's desire to "go out and be united with the stars".

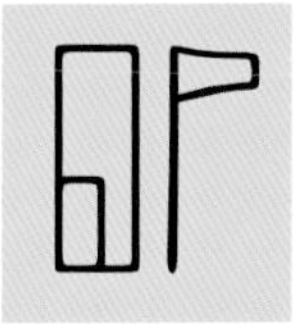

The sign for *ḥwt-nṯr/hewit netcher*, meaning "god's house" or "temple", is composed of the flagpole symbol (representing the flagpoles that decorated temples) together with a rectangular enclosure.

 **Temple**

HOW HIEROGLYPHS WORK

For centuries hieroglyphs were an unbreakable code because scholars were misled by the ancient Egyptians' use of symbols in writing. To break the code modern readers had to understand – as Jean-François Champollion did – that the symbols represent both sounds and ideas (see page 20). The first step of all, however, is to examine how scribes arranged the hieroglyphs.

Ptolemy V (205–180BCE) dedicated this stele to the Buchis bull, venerated at Armant as an embodiment of Montu, god of war. Behind the animal, Montu is represented as a falcon spreading its wings (detail above). Ptolemy V issued the decree inscribed on the Rosetta Stone (see page 11). Here he is depicted presenting the image of three reeds – part of the word for "field" – to the bull, who was associated with fertility and could make the land productive. The inscription states that the incarnation of the Buchis bull commemorated in this stele died in the twenty-fifth year of Ptolemy's reign (181BCE).

THE ARRANGEMENT OF SIGNS

Ancient Egyptian scribes wrote hieroglyphs in both rows and columns with no spaces between the words. Inscriptions can be read from left to right or from right to left along a row and in a column from top to bottom.

When reading a row you can work out in which direction to read because signs containing humans, animals or birds always face toward the beginning of the inscription. For example, when the word for "drink" is written like this , it should be read from the left because the human figure and the bird are facing toward the left. If it is written in this way , it is read from the right.

When a row of hieroglyphs appears vertically reading should begin at the top, for hieroglyphs were never written from the bottom to the top of a column. Within a row if two signs are put together vertically – as the bird and the mouth sign are in "drink" – the upper one should be read first. The signs in "drink" should therefore be read in this order (folded cloth) (sparrow), (mouth), (reed), (water ripples) and (man).

The signs reproduced in this book are printed as we are accustomed to read English – in a straight line from left to right. However, scribes used hieroglyphs as part of the decorative scheme of the monument, tomb or other object on which they were writing, often arranging the signs in the way most pleasing to the eye. When carving an inscription on a monument, they would group the signs to fill the space available. Sometimes they repeated pieces of text in opposing directions for symmetrical effect.

SPELLING AND PRONUNCIATION

This detail from the Karnak inscription shown on page 21 is taken from the line below that reproduced opposite. It is the sign of an owl, shown facing to the right because the Karnak inscription was intended to be read from the right. Its phonetic value was m and it was pronounced "em".

Before Jean-François Champollion made his inspired breakthrough in the decoding of hieroglyphs (see page 11), scholars believed that all hieroglyphic symbols stood for concepts or things and that none was used to represent sounds in the way that the letters of the English alphabet are used. In fact hieroglyphic writing, as Champollion understood, combines ideograms (signs that represent ideas and things) and phonograms (signs that represent sounds).

Many signs depict recognizable creatures or things – for example, (bull), (horse) or (child). Many depict stylized versions of the thing to which they refer, as in (lotus pool), (lotus flower) or (palm branch stripped of leaves). Sometimes a sign is used as the word for the object it depicts. For instance, the word for "mouth" consists of the mouth sign written with a single stroke that indicates, among other things, that this word refers to the thing that is represented. Similarly the words for "sun" and "arm" are written with the signs that represent those objects. More usually, however, hieroglyphic signs represent sounds in the Egyptian language – they are used as phonograms. Two picture signs representing different sounds can be put together to make a new word, which often has nothing to do with the things represented by the picture signs themselves. A hypothetical English equivalent usually quoted by scholars would be to write "belief" by combining the images of a bee and a tree's leaf: bee-leaf. If you were trying to decode this hypothetical English hieroglyph and expected the resulting word to relate to bees, leaves, honey or trees, you would be heading in entirely the wrong direction.

By careful comparison of the use of hieroglyphic signs in different contexts, scholars have identified specific signs with individual sounds. Where possible they have matched these sounds with the letters of the English alphabet. But some sounds in ancient Egyptian do not have exact equivalents in English and so cannot be represented using letters of the alphabet; in these cases scholars have developed a set of signs to represent the sounds (see pages 22–23). The translation of hieroglyphic pictures into sounds is called "transliteration". Ancient Egyptian hieroglyphs did not represent vowel sounds (a,e,i,o,u) and so only consonants are used in transliteration.

In the word for "house", the rectangle represents a house; the pronunciation of the word combined the conso-

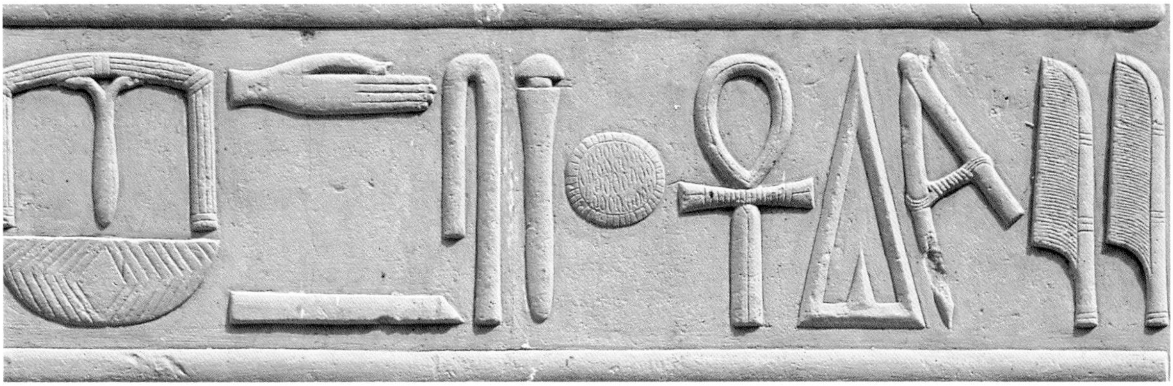

The lefthand section of this hieroglyphic relief from the White Chapel of the Twelfth-Dynasty king Senwosret I (1919–1875BCE) at Karnak reads, as detailed from right to left below, "given life [on] the first day [of] the Sed festival". This festival was held – typically after thirty years of the king's reign – to reinvigorate his power to rule.

nant sounds p and r – and the sign is transliterated using those letters: *pr*. The word for "to go forth" made the same sound combination. In this context the sign of the house works to represent the sound combination *pr(i)*; the mouth sign reinforces this, because it represents the sound *r*; the sign for walking legs helps to distinguish between the house symbol used as an ideogram in and the same symbol used as a phonogram in "to go forth" – the leg sign indicates that the word is to do with movement and is an example of a determinative (see page 24).

Scholars do not know for certain how the ancient Egyptians pronounced the words represented by hieroglyphs, but they have a good idea based on comparative research in Coptic (see page 13). As well as transliterating hieroglyphic signs into recognizable letters (but using only consonants), we can write out the word's probable pronunciation complete with vowel sounds. The word house , transliterated *pr*, was probably pronounced "pair". In this book the hieroglyphic words cited are followed firstly by the transliteration, then the pronunciation, thus: "house" *pr/pair*; "mistress of the house" *nbt-pr/nebet -pair*; the ancient name for Egypt ("the black land") *kmt/Kemet*.

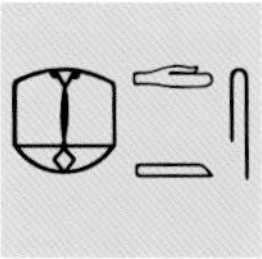

THE HAND D, UNKNOWN SIGN AND FOLDED CLOTH S SPELL SD/SED; THE LEFT SIGN IS ḤB/HEB "FESTIVAL".

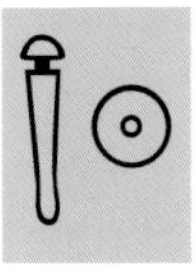

THE DAGGER SIGN TP/TEP MEANS "FIRST" AND THE SUN SYMBOL HRW/HEROO MEANS "DAY".

THE ANKH SIGN ʿNH/ANNK, TOGETHER WITH A CONICAL LOAF Di/DEE MEANS "GIVEN LIFE".

THE ALPHABET

This "scarab" – so called because the reverse side is fashioned in the form of a scarab beetle – is one of a pair issued by Amenhotep III in the tenth year of his reign (c.1380BCE). The inscription lists the royal titles of the king and his queen, then states "the number of lions that his majesty killed with his own arrows from Year 1 to Year 10: 102 wild lions". Letters of the alphabet – as shown in the box (right) – are detailed in the annotation.

Ancient Egyptian used a standard alphabet of twenty-four "letters" each of which represented a single consonant. The letters are shown in the box below alongside their transliteration (see pages 20–21) – either a letter from the English alphabet or a transliteration sign devised by scholars – and their probable pronunciation.

The sounds represented by the transliteration signs given in the alphabet box below are as follows: *3* – glottal stop, similar to "thro'le" (for "throttle") in Cockney English; *i* – like "y"; *ʿ* – guttural "ah" sound; *ḥ* – emphatic "h"; *ḫ* – similar to "ch" in Scottish "loch"; *ẖ* – similar to "ch" in German "ich"; *š* – "sh" as in "shimmy"; *ḳ* – "kw" like "q" in "queen"; *ṯ* – similar to to "t" in "tube"; *ḏ* – "dj" similar to "j" in "joker".

The language also used a number of signs that represented combinations of two consonants (these are known as "biliteral signs") or combinations of three consonants (known as "triliteral signs"). A list of biliteral signs and a selection of triliteral signs is given on pages 158–9 in the Reference File section at the end of this book.

THE BASIC ALPHABET OF 24 SINGLE-CONSONANT LETTERS

SIGN	TRANSLITERATION	OBJECT SHOWN	PRONUNCIATION
𓄿	*3*	Egyptian vulture	*glottal stop*
𓇋	*i*	flowering reed	*y*
𓇌 or \\	*y*	two reed flowers or two strokes	*y*
𓂝	*ʿ*	forearm	*guttural ah*
𓅱	*w*	quail chick	*w/u*
𓃀	*b*	foot	*b*
𓊪	*p*	stool	*p*
𓆑	*f*	horned viper	*f*
𓅓	*m*	owl	*m*
𓈖	*n*	water ripple	*n*
𓂋	*r*	mouth	*r*
𓉔	*h*	reed shelter in fields	*h*
𓎛	*ḥ*	twisted flax	*emphatic h*

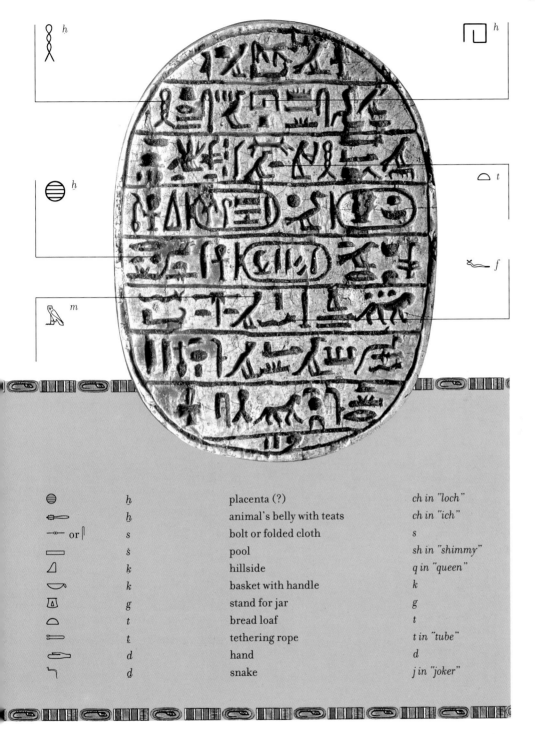

	ḫ	placenta (?)	*ch in "loch"*
	ẖ	animal's belly with teats	*ch in "ich"*
or	s	bolt or folded cloth	*s*
	š	pool	*sh in "shimmy"*
	ḳ	hillside	*q in "queen"*
	k	basket with handle	*k*
	g	stand for jar	*g*
	t	bread loaf	*t*
	ṯ	tethering rope	*t in "tube"*
	d	hand	*d*
	ḏ	snake	*j in "joker"*

DETERMINATIVES

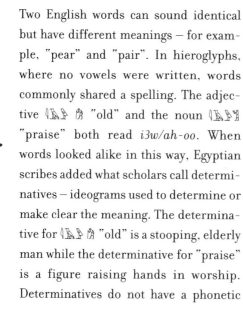

A detail from the copy of the tomb painting shown opposite shows Osiris wearing the plumed atef crown that was one of his identifying marks. Osiris also wears the long, curved beard associated with kings and gods; the beard is visible on the determinative used for god and king words (see right).

Two English words can sound identical but have different meanings – for example, "pear" and "pair". In hieroglyphs, where no vowels were written, words commonly shared a spelling. The adjective "old" and the noun "praise" both read *i3w/ah-oo*. When words looked alike in this way, Egyptian scribes added what scholars call determinatives – ideograms used to determine or make clear the meaning. The determinative for "old" is a stooping, elderly man while the determinative for "praise" is a figure raising hands in worship. Determinatives do not have a phonetic function – they represent no sound. Ideograms of a man or parts of the male anatomy including the penis and were used to determine words with male aspects: for example, *s3/sar* "son" and *h3y/hay* "husband". Ideograms of a woman were used to determine words with female aspects such as *mwt/moot* "mother".

Some determinatives were linked only to one word while others could be used with a range of words, giving a general sense of the meaning. Scholars call the second type "generic determinatives"; a list of common examples is given below.

GENERIC DETERMINATIVES

- man
- woman
- god
- eat, drink, speak, think, feel
- enemy, foreigner
- high, rejoice
- eye, see
- offer, present
- walk, run
- turn backward
- limb, flesh
- cattle
- bird
- sky, above
- sun, light, time
- night, darkness
- air, wind, sail
- house
- town, village
- boat, ship
- clothe, linen
- bread, cake
- vine, fruit, garden
- festival
- mummy, likeness
- small, bad, weak

A nineteenth-century CE copy of a tomb painting in the tomb of Sety I (1290–1279BCE) shows Osiris enthroned; some determinatives are detailed below.

1 A SIGN RESEMBLING A CIRCLE AND CROSS WAS THE DETERMINATIVE FOR NAMES OF TOWNS OR COUNTRIES.

2 A SEATED FIGURE WITH A BEARD WAS THE DETERMINATIVE FOR NAMES OF GODS (SEE PAGE 89).

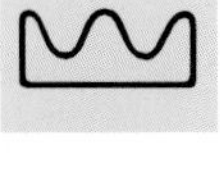

3 A SCHEMATIC REPRESENTATION OF A ROW OF HILLS DETERMINED WORDS LINKED TO THE WEST OR FOREIGN LANDS.

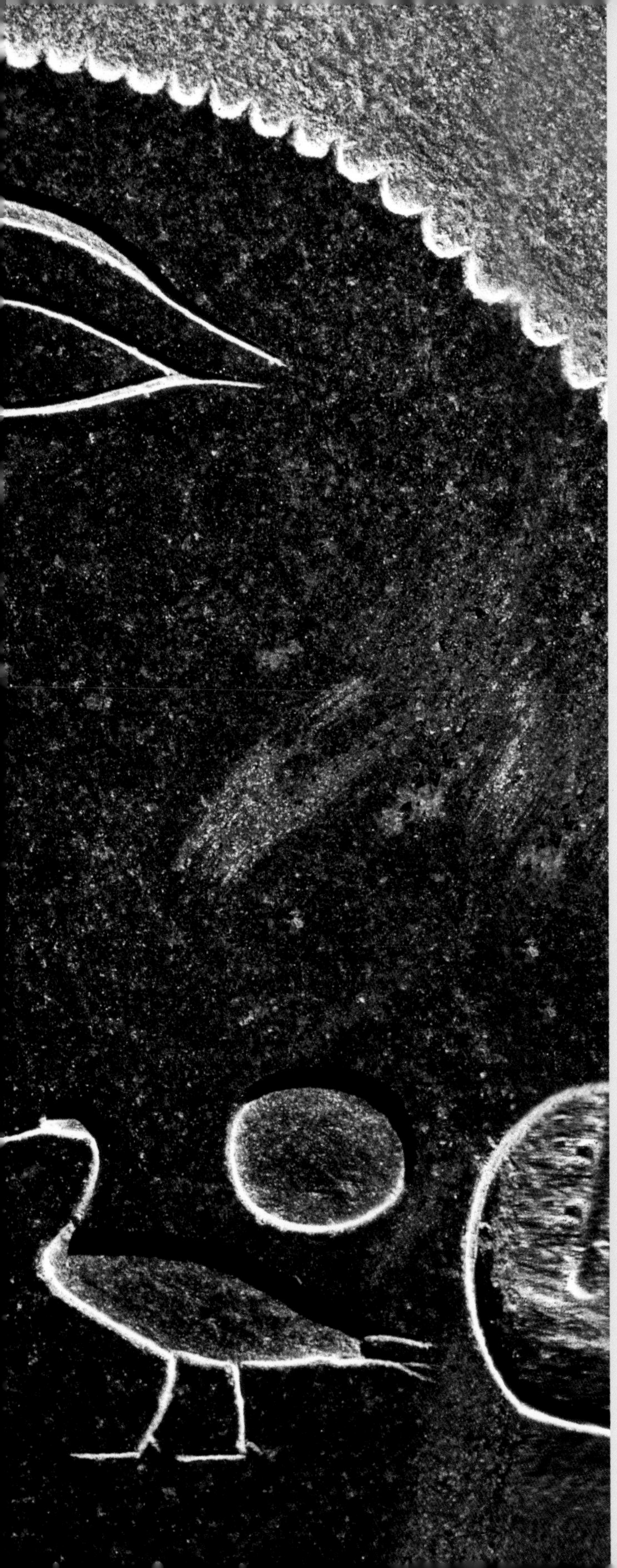

CHAPTER TWO

ORIGINS OF THE SIGNS

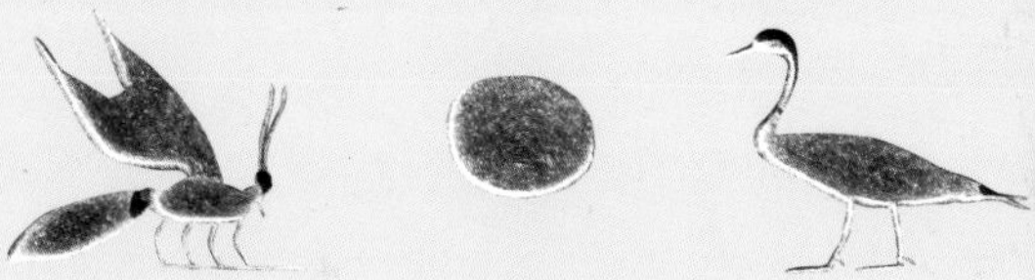

The world of the ancient Egyptians stands revealed in their hieroglyphs. The symbols of hieroglyphic writing include images not only of the animals and birds with which the Egyptians shared the land, but also the temples, houses, tombs and granaries they built, the tools they used to work the fields and the containers in which they stored their food and drink.

The words "King of Upper and Lower Egypt", "Son of Re" and "beautiful things" can be read in this obelisk carving of c.1800BCE from Dashur.

SIGNS FROM NATURE

Fishermen haul in an oversized catch in a river teeming with wildlife. The image is from the tomb of the sculptor Ipi at Deir el Medina. The Egyptians often regarded the marshy river borders as places of ill omen, home of evil spirits.

The Egyptians depended on the Nile for the fertility of their land, but could never predict how widely the river would flood in the next inundation. Uncertainty dominated the Egyptian world-view: the people saw that health, family life and prosperity were governed by erratic environmental factors.

ON THE BANKS OF THE NILE

Hieroglyphic signs that relate to the natural world often act alone and provide clear visual reference. Examples include 𓇋 *i*, which represents a flowering reed, , reeds growing side by side, 𓃗, a horse, and , an ostrich. Animal signs were often used as determinatives for words denoting emotions or activities that the Egyptians linked with a particular species – the crocodile, for example, was associated with both aggression and terror. The sudden appearance from the water of the crocodile with gaping jaws understandably inspired terror in the Egyptians. In

tomb paintings showing the test in the underworld Hall of Judgment at which the heart of the deceased was weighed against the feather of the goddess Maat, representing truth (see pages 72, 88 and 100), "the devourer" who awaited those who failed the test was often shown with crocodile head and lion's body. The crocodile symbol also served in the name of the crocodile god *sbk/Sobek*.

Certain fish were considered by the ancient Egyptians to be unclean – and for this reason could not be offered to priests or to the king. One of the signs for fish was the determinative in the word *bwt/boot* which means "abomination". Nevertheless, the majority of people regularly ate fish. A particular type of fish *int/ent* (*Tilapia nilotica*, known in Arabic as *bulti*) appears – doubtless due to its red colour – to have been associated with the Sun. Moreover, because the *bulti*'s offspring can be seen to emerge from its mouth, where it has incubated and hatched them, the fish became, alongside the lotus flower (see box, page 40), a symbol of rebirth.

The frog, so numerous in the wild, was associated with fertility and Heket, goddess of childbirth. The hieroglyphic symbol of the frog was the determinative in the goddess's name *ḥkt/heket*. The goddess was often represented by the frog symbol alone.

The cobra was associated with the king, the sun and the kingdom of Lower Egypt from early predynastic times onward. After the unification of Egypt the cobra appeared as the symbol of the snake goddess Wadjet (representing Lower Egypt) alongside the image of the vulture goddess Nekhbet (Upper Egypt) in the king's "Two Ladies" name *nbty/nebti*. (see also page 6). A rearing cobra – later called *uraeus* by the ancient Greeks – often appeared in a protective function on the king's crown (see page 98).

The duck was sometimes viewed as representing the evil spirits of the marshes, but was treated at other times as a symbol of fertility. Two common hieroglyphic forms of the duck were , the pintail duck symbol, and , the same duck flying, which appeared in the word p3/par "to fly".

BODIES HUMAN AND DIVINE

Representations of the wedjat or eye of the falcon god Horus vary, but many appear to represent a human eye (above), while others seem to depict a falcon's eye. The wedjat opposite dates from the Third Intermediate Period (1075–656BCE).

The ancient Egyptians developed a sound knowledge of human anatomy through the practice of mummification (see page 96); they were familiar with the major organs of the body and the brain, and, to some extent, with their function. It is not surprising, therefore, that images of the body were incorporated into Egyptian symbolic representation.

In mythology Horus, the falcon-headed god, was the symbol of divine kingship. Early myths tell of an eye injury sustained by Horus during a battle with his uncle Seth: the goddess Hathor used a potion of gazelle milk to restore the eye, which was later revered as a sacred symbol and associated with the healing arts. In hieroglyphic texts the eye of Horus symbol *wḏ3t/wedjat* is translated as "whole". In another myth Horus's eye shattered into many pieces when Seth tore it out and hurled it away, but the ibis-headed god Thoth collected them and restored them to wholeness. The eyes of Horus were often associated with the sun and the moon, and scholars believe that Egyptians understood the story of the injury and recovery of the eye to describe the waxing and waning of the Moon (see also pages 146–147).

The eye of Horus was often worn in the form of a pendant or amulet. In New Kingdom (1539–1075BCE) images, the *wedjat* was often shown with wings, hovering protectively behind the king. In hieroglyphic writing a less elaborate depiction of the eye was used to denote the human organ and its function . Other eye signs included , the eye decorated with eye paint, and , the eye with a painted lower lid. A weeping eye was the determinative for the verb "to weep" *rmi/remi* (see page 106). Another image of the eye with eyepaint was the determinative for the word "sleep" *ʿʿwy/oo-way*.

The sign of the phallus or often determined words that related to men and male activity – it was the determinative in the words "husband" and "son" (see page 24) and in *nk/nek* "copulate" (see also pages 108–109). It was also determinative for the word "bull" , an animal that the ancient Egyptians revered as a symbol of fertility, prowess and regeneration (see page 34).

The phallus was associated with early myths. The body of Osiris, murdered by his brother Seth, was dismembered and thrown into the Nile. Isis, the sister-wife of Osiris, collected and assembled the remains of her husband and thereby created the first mummy. She used her magic to activate the body of Osiris and make

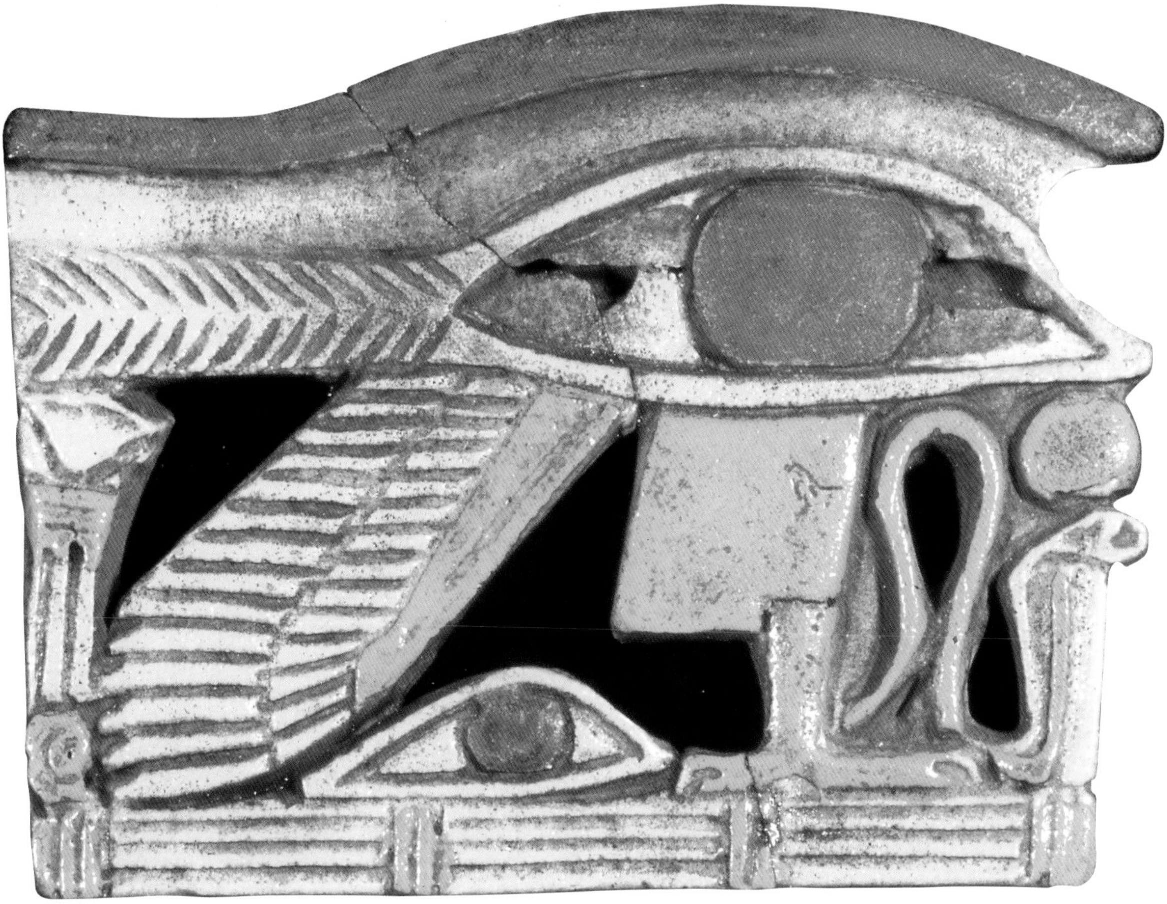

As a symbol of healing and wholeness, the wedjat, or eye of Horus, was worn as a protective amulet by the living and was placed among the wrappings of the mummified corpse. People also painted the wedjat on the bows of boats.

him sexually potent. Phallic imagery was emphasized in artistic representations of this important Egyptian myth, which was often portrayed on temple walls.

The backbone may have been the object represented by the djed column that became a potent symbol of stability for the Egyptians. The djed is a vertical column with horizontal strips toward the top (see reproduction on page 32) and in hieroglyphic writing was represented by 𓊽. Some scholars have seen it as a rendering of a stake with sheaves of grain tied to it. In the Old Kingdom (2625–2130BCE), the djed was associated with Ptah the creator, according to the mythology of Memphis, but the column increasingly became linked to Osiris and by the New Kingdom was used as a symbol of that god, often identified with his backbone. In New Kingdom coffins the djed symbol was painted on the inner part of the coffin

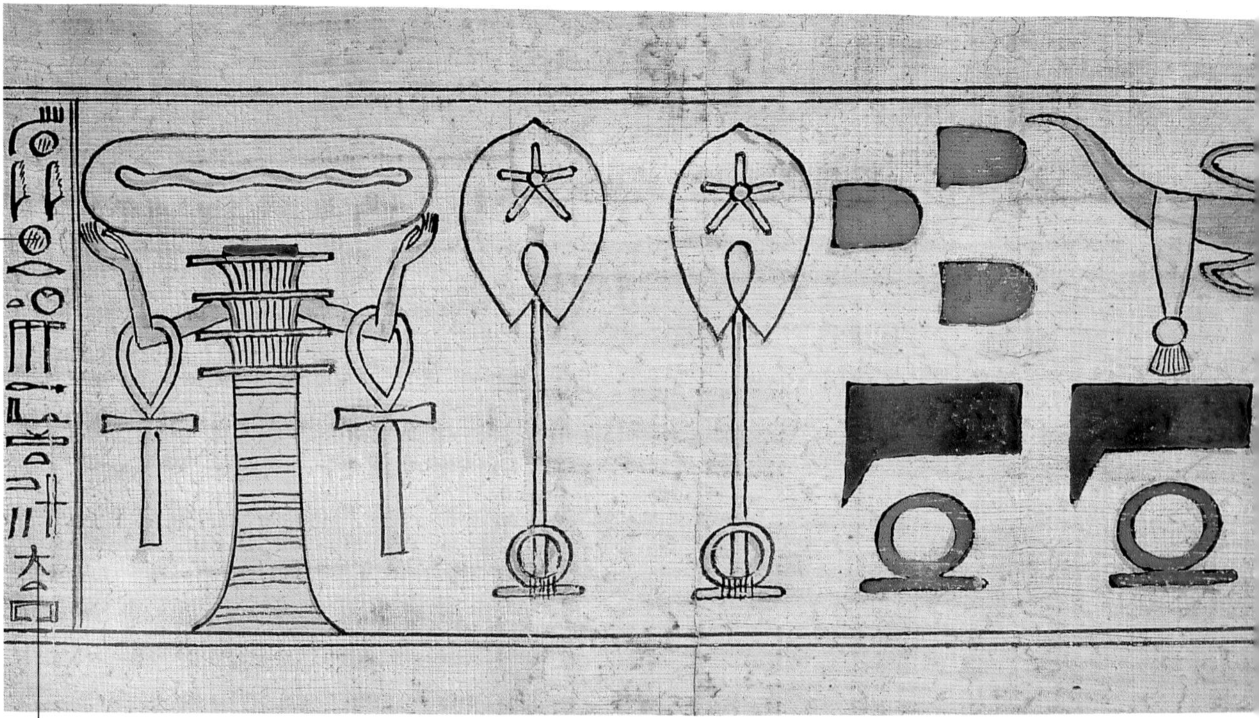

2 The Underworld

1 Gods' things

The djed pillar – thought to represent the spinal column – is depicted with human arms holding the ankh or sign of life in this vignette from the Book of the Dead. This book belonged to Chensumose, a Twenty-First Dynasty (1075-945BCE) priest.

bottom, where the back of the mummy would lie – symbolically identifying the deceased with Osiris.

The djed column was also associated with kingship. Some scholars believe that an ancient ceremony involving the djed column was performed at the start of each royal reign, when, using ropes and with the help of priests, the king would erect a large djed column. The ceremony probably symbolized the continuity and stability that ran from the previous reign to the new one and also celebrated the birth to new life in the underworld of the deceased king. It may also have recalled the return to life of Osiris in early myth.

The hieroglyphic words for "arm" *ʿ/ah* and for "head" *tp/tep* include representations of the forearm and of the human head in profile. The sign of the forearm had a phonetic function in many words as the sound represented by the transliteration sign ʿ – a guttural sound unknown in English (see pages 22-23). It also appeared in the word for the Egyptian unit of measurement known as the "cubit" – around 20 inches (50cm) and reckoned to be average distance between elbow and fingertips (see pages 142–143). The word cubit *mḥ/mer* was sometimes written . In various contexts, the forearm was depicted holding objects including a rounded bread loaf, a stick, a bowl and a sceptre. For example, it appears holding a stick in one variant of the verb "to hunt" *bḥs/bee-hess* and in a variant of the verb "to snare birds" *sẖt/sek-et*. It also appears in this form in the verb "to embalm" *sdwẖ/seddoak* (see page 64) and the word for "soldier" *wꜥw/oaho* (see page 120).

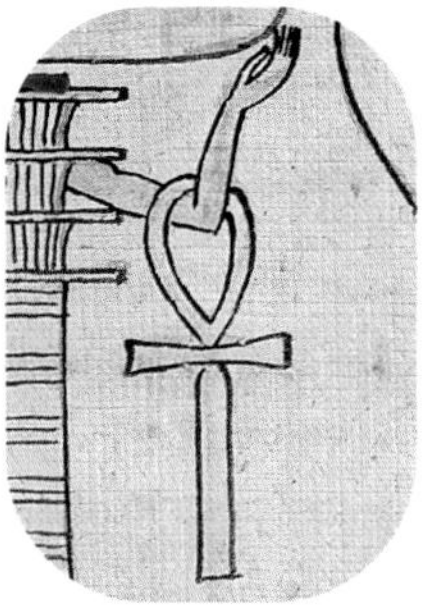

A detail of the eye, cheek and nose in profile was the determinative in the word for "nose" *fnd/fend*. The same symbol was represented in the word or *sn/sen*, meaning "to kiss" (see pages 108–109) and was a generic determinative (see pages 24–25) for words associated with joy as well as those linked to the action of smelling. The hieroglyphic word for "body" *ẖt/het* combined a sign thought to represent the body of an animal showing tail and teats, with a bread loaf (phonetic *t*) and a single stroke. The determinative in the word for "tooth" *ibḥ/eber* is a sign thought to represent an elephant tusk.

A pair of arms was the determinative for the verb "to embrace" *ink/enk*. This word was sometimes used in contexts where it meant "to envelop". In the Middle Kingdom (1980–1630BCE), statues of family groups regularly depicted a father with arms reaching down to touch the child standing before him in such a way that his arms matched the shape of the embrace sign. Sometimes, too, statuary of Isis holding her son Horus before her showed the goddess's arms taking this shape. A similar symbol was used in the word for *ka* or spirit *k3/car* (see page 100).

The symbol of the walking legs was the generic determinative for words associated with walking, running or linked activities – for example, another variant of the verb "to hunt" *bḥs/bee-hess* and the word for "military expedition" *wḏyt/wajeet*. Another representation of the leg and foot was used to determine words associated with these body parts.

The sign for hair is clearly derived from artistic representations of the hairpieces worn by many ancient Egyptians. During funerary rites, it was customary for a wealthy Egyptian family to hire professional mourners. As a sign of grief, the mourners would weep loudly and tear at their hair while they followed the catafalque bearing the body of the dead individual. The hair sign as a determinative is not only applicable to the word "hair", it also determines words such as *ẖ3rt/hart* or *ẖ3rt/hart* "widow" – both of which also use the female determinative sign – and *i3kb/eakheb* the verb "to mourn".

The text shown opposite from Chensumose's Book of the Dead is only a fragment and cannot be translated into a comprehensible sentence. Details are explained below.

1 SPELLS NṮR-W/NETCHER-OO "GODS". SIGNS FOR THE PLACENTA, THE MOUTH AND THE BREAD LOAF SPELL ẖRT/HURT "THINGS"; THE SUN SYMBOL IS THE DETERMINATIVE. THE WHOLE SPELLS "GODS' THINGS".

2 THE STAR SYMBOL AND THE BREAD LOAF SPELL SB3T/SABAT, THE UNDERWORLD. THE HOUSE SYMBOL IS USED AS THE DETERMINATIVE SIGN, BECAUSE THE WORD DESCRIBES THE DWELLING-PLACE OF OSIRIS.

THE ANIMAL WORLD

Agriculture was the source of ancient Egypt's prosperity – animals were widely used for transport and provided food for wealthy Egyptians. The number of cattle owned by a household was a clear indication of the value of the estate. The sign for "cattle" *mnmnt/menment* is determined by a horned cow, beneath which are strokes that emphasize the plural nature of the word – "cattle herd".

Yet while people valued animals as allies, they also saw them as potential enemies – for the Egyptians lived in fear of man-hunting beasts and reptiles. Because hieroglyphic signs could be animated through magic and ritual (see page 63), the Egyptians considered signs containing images of some wild animals or reptiles to be dangerous. When used in religious writings, the figures of animals were sometimes "disempowered" by being shown bound or beheaded.

Animals played an important role in religious and cultural life. Bulls were venerated and believed to contain the force and essence of deities – the sacred bull of Apis at Memphis, for example, was held to be the embodiment of Ptah in life and of Osiris in death; and the bull worshipped at Armant embodied Montu, god of war (see page 19). Animal sacrifice was a central part of

The cattle count – held every two years – was an important domestic event on farming estates. Wooden models depicting the count were carved for the Middle Kingdom Theban tomb of Meketre (c.2000BCE). The head of the household sits on the podium with his son and four scribes.

the temple rituals designed to promote the soil's fertility, and animal determinatives are often included in words that denote sacrificial practices. Sacred bulls and lions, symbolic of fertility and strength, were used in royal names and titles associated with authority. The king could be celebrated as "strong bull"; and the word for "hereditary prince" or "mayor" *ḥ3ty-ꜥ/harty-ah* contains an image of the head and paws of a lion.

Animal signs were also used to indicate qualities associated with a species. The symbol for a tadpole was used as the hieroglyph for the number 100,000 (see page 142).

ANIMAL ALLIES AND ENEMIES

CAT *miw/meow* The last sign in the word for cat is the determinative (hide with tail) often used in animal names. The pronunciation mimicked the cat's cry. The creature was domesticated from the Middle Kingdom (1980–1630BCE) onward to keep rodents and snakes at bay in houses.

MONKEY *ky/kee* One variant of the word for "monkey" contains the image of a baboon that the Egyptians held to be sacred.

CROCODILE *msḥ/mesh* This word consists of an owl (*m*), a bolt (*s*) and a twisted flax (*ḥ*). It is determined by the sign of a crocodile.

SNAKE *hf3w/hefaroo* The ancient Egyptians saw the snake as a dangerous reptile and greatly feared its bite. Images of various species of snake appear in hieroglyphic words – here the likeness of a cobra is used as the determinative of the general word for snake.

HOSTS OF THE AIR

The ancient Egyptians built their towns and cities close to the water sources that they shared with the animal, reptile and bird populations and, often encountering birds in the wild, became intimately acquainted with their behaviour. The erratic movements of a large bird population seemed to the Egyptians the ultimate image of chaos; by contrast, they used the representation of netted birds as a symbol of nature controlled.

Bird images appeared in many hieroglyphic words, and often a similar sign was used as determinative for both negative and positive words. For example, a sparrow with its tail feather pointing downward determined words such as *bin/been* "bad", while a sparrow with a slightly more squared and upright tail determined positive words such as *wr/wier* "great". The symbol of the vulture, similarly, was used in both *nrw/neroo* "terror" and *mwt/moot* "mother". While the Egyptians associated the vulture with terror because it ate the flesh of the dead, they linked it with maternal instincts, too, because they had seen how well the female vulture cared for her young. The vulture was also associated with several goddesses including Mut (the consort of Amun) and Nekhbet, the national goddess of Upper Egypt (see also pages 6 and 29).

The Egyptians had many sky gods in their pantheon: in the Pyramid Texts (see pages 70–71) there are references to a

SELECTED BIRD SIGNS

BIRD *3pd/aped* The ancient Egyptians used a large and varied number of bird species in their hieroglyphic signs. The symbols for vulture and goose are both used here – the vulture (*3*), the stool (*p*) and the hand (*d*) spell the word and the goose is the determinative sign. The words for "bird" and "goose" were both spelled *3pd* and were interchangeable in use.

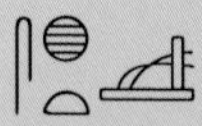

TO SNARE *sḫt/sek-et* A folded linen cloth (*s*), a placenta (*ḫ*) and a bread loaf sign (*t*) spell *sḫt*. The determinative is the image of a bird trap.

FLY *p3/pa* The verb "to fly" consists of a stool (*p*), a flying duck (*p3*) – which reinforces the *pa* sound – and a vulture (*3*); the word is determined by a bird's wing.

1 Owl sign, used with a sceptre to form a word meaning "power"

2 Quail chick, used beneath a sail: the word as a whole means "breath"

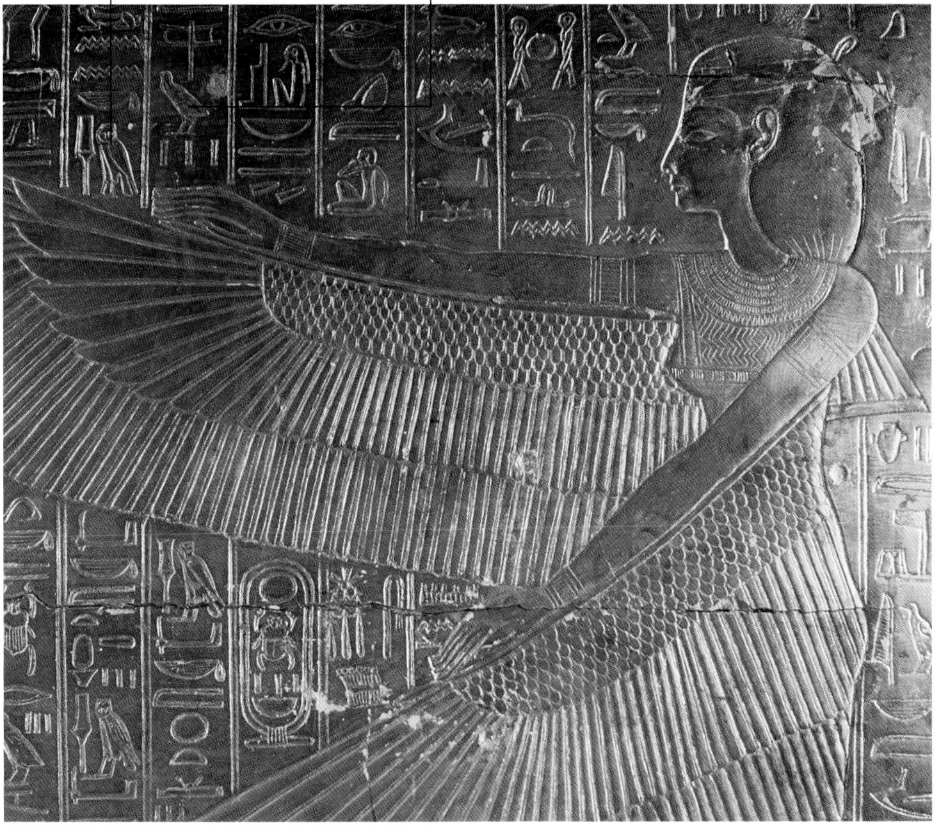

The goddess Isis spreads protective wings in a carving from the shrine of Tutankhamun (c.1332–1322BCE). The symbols for the quail chick and owl appear in the inscription.

1 The symbol for the owl (m) was used as m in mʿr/mar "happy", smr/semer "courtier", hmhmt/hem-het "war cry" and kmt/kemet, "Egypt".

2 The symbol of the quail chick served as phonetic w. It was used as w in the words for "river" jtrw/eat-roo, "breeze" swt/soot and "food" šbw/sheboo.

primeval time when "the sky was separated from the Earth, when the gods ascended to the sky." If depicted in art with a sun disc on his head, the falcon was the sun god Re-Horakhty. Most often in hieroglyphic writing the image of the falcon referred to Horus, the god incarnated in each reigning pharaoh (see page 82).

Birds were frequently associated with protective forces. The king was often shown embraced and protected by the wings of a bird, while winged goddesses were sometimes placed at each corner of the king's coffin.

Despite the fact that certain birds were the living image of gods and goddesses, the Egyptians – both upper and lower classes – enjoyed eating them. In tomb pantings tables are often shown heaped with geese, duck and guinea fowl.

REEDS AND FLOWERS

Stylized carvings of the papyrus and lotus – the heraldic plants of Upper and Lower Egypt – adorn granite pillars in the temple of Amun Re at Karnak in Luxor. Egyptologists call the surrounding area of the temple the "botanical gardens" because it contains wall reliefs showing plants brought back to Egypt following the foreign campaigns of Tuthmosis III (c.1479–1425BCE).

The papyrus plant grew prolifically in the north and came to be associated with that area. A thicket of papyri was used in the word for "north" (Lower Egypt or the Delta) *t3-mhw/taa mahoo*. Similarly the word for south *rswt/resoot* contained the sign for the sedge plant because that plant grew there. The same sedge plant sign was also used in *rsyw/resoo* ("southerners") and *sm'w/shemoo* ("Upper Egypt").

The Egyptians prized exotic plants and flowers. In the course of foreign military expeditions, a wide range of tree and plant species were recorded – and some were transported back to Egypt. Flowers were highly valued as objects of personal adornment. At official banquets (see page 56) necklaces of flowers were given to guests, and garlands were placed on food platters and decorative stands. The Egyptian upper classes often maintained private gardens. The garden, which was often represented on the walls of private tombs, became a symbol of opulence and luxury. Large gardens were sometimes attached to vineyards and orchards. Many garden designs incorporated pools, and had courtyards that were shaded with trees or palms.

Plants and flowers were not simply a luxury – they were put to many uses. Oils and perfumes were used in cosmetics; camomile and cedar oils were a good

PLANTS AND GARDENS

LOTUS POOL *š3/shar* The sign has a pool with lotus flowers, shown both open and in bud.

GARDEN *ḫnt-š/hent-esh* The sign of three water pots in a rack had the phonetic value *ḫnt*. In the word for "garden" the *n* value is reinforced by the water ripple and the *t* by the bread loaf sign. The pool symbol provides the sound *š/esh*.

EMMER WHEAT *bdt/bedet* The foot (*b*), hand (*d*) and loaf (*t*) spell *bdt*; the determinative is the image of a bearded ear of emmer wheat.

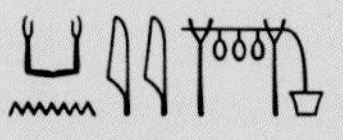

GARDENER *k3ny/karny* The word for "gardener" shows a vine propped on twin supports. The same vine symbol was used as the determinative in *irp/urp*, the word for "wine".

insect-repellent. Plant extracts were also used in embalming. Priests used flowers, incense and plant derivatives in temple ritual (see pages 112–114). As a result signs representing plants were used as ideograms in words associated with worship and temple life – for example, the sign representing a reed appears in slightly modified form in "offering piles" *ꜥ3bt/ah-bet*; scholars believe the crisscross lines in this sign represent conical cakes given as offerings. Flowers were placed in tombs as a symbol of regeneration. Wreaths of olive leaves, papyrus and small blue cornflowers were found among the coffins of Tutankhamun (*c*.1332–1322BCE) in his Valley of the Kings tomb. The lotus flower was a symbol of new life (see box, below).

Plant signs were used as determinatives in words associated with growth and youth. The sign representing a palm branch stripped of leaves was used in the word *rnpi/renpee* meaning "youthful" or "vigorous"; similarly the symbol for flower was used in the word *ḥwn/hewn* "to be young". The palm branch sign was also used in words that expressed concepts of time and its measurement – for example, in "year" *rnpt/renpet* and – in a slightly different form – in "season" *tr/tre*.

Plant signs were also, understandably enough, used in words associated with the countryside. The sign for the reed appeared in or "marshland" *sḫt/seket*, in *sḫt/seket* "field" and in "peasant" *sḫty/sek-ety*.

FLOWER OF MANY MEANINGS

The lotus had an important symbolic role in religious life. The blue lotus, which opens with the first rays of the sun, and the white lotus, which opens only at night, were associated with the sun and moon, and the opposing forces of light and dark.

In the first days, according to one creation myth, the sun god Re was born from a lotus flower that floated on the waters of eternity. The lotus became a symbol of rebirth after death. An object found in the tomb of Tutankhamun (*c*.1332–1322BCE) shows the head of the king emerging from a lotus. One surviving magic formula from the Book of the Dead was for the transformation of the deceased into a lotus flower: "I am this pure lotus flower that has ascended by the sunlight and is at the nose of the sun god Re."

Because of its association with new life, the lotus was linked to fertility and was a sexual symbol. In tomb art, women were often depicted inhaling the fragrance of the lotus flower at banquets.

THE DIVINE ELEMENTS OF LIFE

Ancient Egyptian creation myths told how in the first days of the world life emerged from the primeval waters of chaos, called "Nun". Earth rose from the waters to form the original island of creation (see page 145). The Egyptians were inspired in this mythology by the mounds of fertile earth seemingly left behind by the Nile each year after the river had flooded – mounds that appeared to rise from the retreating waters. According to one of the creation myths told in Heliopolis in Lower Egypt, the god Atum *'tm/atum* came forth from the waters of chaos and the sun god Re emerged from a lotus flower at the first sunrise. Without the sunlight there would be no life in the Nile's riverbanks, however fertile they were, and Atum was understood to be the source of all – his name meant "whole". When Atum was shown as a human male wearing the crowns of Upper and Lower Egypt (see page 86), he represented the setting sun.

Atum created Shu (god of air) and Tefnut (goddess of moisture), who coupled to produce *gb/Geb* the earth god and *nwt/Nut* the sky goddess. They in turn parented *Wsir/Osiris*, *s(w)th/Seth* (gods of order and disorder) and their consorts *3st/Isis*, and Nepthys. These nine gods and goddesses,

A page from the Book of the Dead of the scribe Ani depicts (top left corner) one of the underworld lakes of fire that received the souls of the damned.

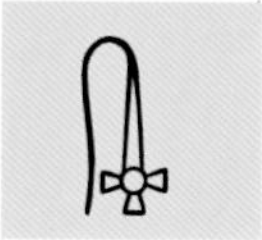

THE LAKE IS SURROUNDED BY FOUR BRAZIER SIGNS, INDICATING ITS FIERY CONTENTS; THE BRAZIER SIGN DETERMINED WORDS LINKED TO FIRE.

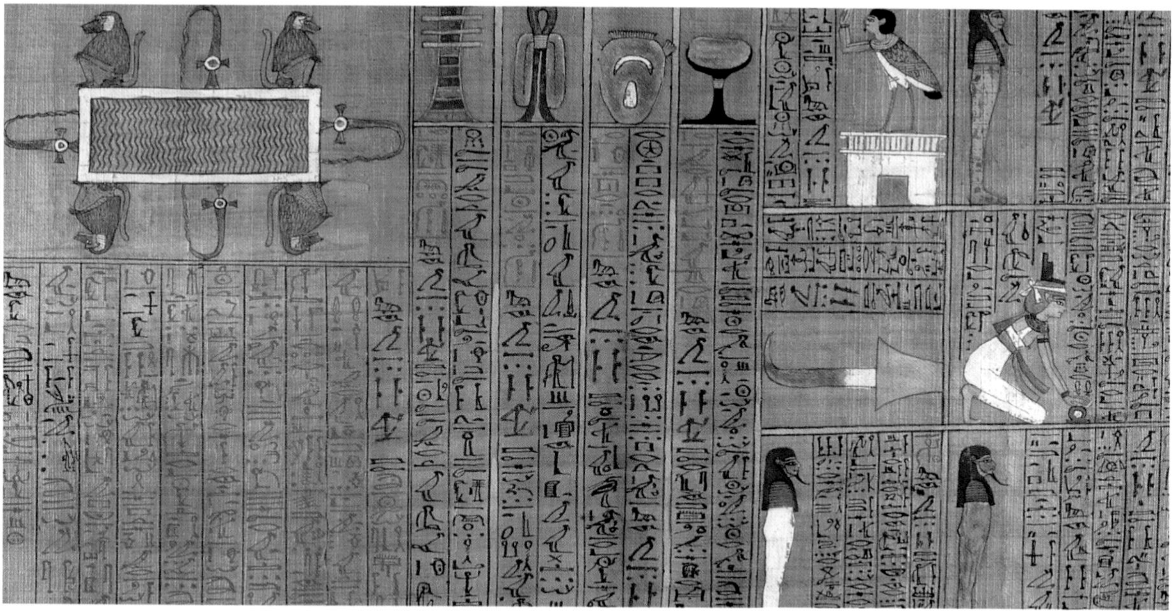

Tomb

worshipped at Heliopolis, were later called the *Ennead* (Group of Nine) by ancient Greek writers.

The fertility of the Earth was inextricably linked to Osiris, a nature god by whose resurrection all living things were thought to thrive. Seeds were often placed in planting beds that were designed in the distinctive shape of the body of this god. Known as Osiris beds, these were placed in the tomb, where they symbolized the regeneration of life. The flooding of the Nile was personified in the androgynous god Hapi, who was represented as a man with pendulous breasts; the coming of the flood was often called "the arrival of Hapi". He was said to live in a cavern at the southern border of Egypt. The hieroglyphic word for "earth" *t3/tar* depicts an area of cultivated land. The word for water *mw/moo* consists of three wavy lines that depict a water current. The word for the season of the inundation (see pages 140–141) *3ẖt/ar-ket* depicts a pool with a series of plants (together with a placenta and a bread loaf).

The Egyptians had little scientific concept of the effects of air on the human body, but they were aware of the importance and function of the lungs. Of all the religious rites that were performed on the dead, the ceremony of opening the mouth was the most important. A special instrument called an *adze* was used to open the mouth of the mummy, and in this way to reanimate the deceased. The spirit of the deceased was released from the body in the form of the Ba, often shown as a human-headed bird. One spell from the Book of the Dead, entitled "A Spell for Giving Breath in the Realm of the Dead", invokes the god of air: "I am Shu who draws the air into the presence of the sunshine to the limits of the sky, to the limits of the earth, to the limits of the plume of the nebeh-bird, and air is given to those youths who open my mouth so that I may see with my eyes." The verb "to breathe" *ssn/sesen* or *tpi/tepi* was determined with the symbol of the human eye and nose. The word for "breath" *ṯ3w/che-ah-o* combined the images of a sail and a quail chick. The sail symbol was a generic determinative for words to do with air, wind or sails – for example, "breeze" (see box below). It was an ideogram in the words for "north wind", "sail" and "skipper" *nfw/nefoo*.

The Egyptians generally regarded fire as an evil force and believed that in the underworld the deceased had to beware of lakes of fire. The Book of the Dead equipped the deceased with spells with which to avoid being burnt or scorched. One reads: "O Bull of the West, I am brought to you, for I am that oar of Re with which the Old Ones are rowed. I will be neither burnt up nor scorched, for I am Babai, the eldest son of Osiris, for whom all the gods have assembled within his Eye in Heliopolis."

Amenhotep IV (c.1353–1336 BCE), also called Akhenaten, worships light emitted by the Aten (sun disc) in this relief. Hieroglyphs to the left of the sun spell "tomb" (below).

(SUN ON THE HORIZON) *3ḪT* AND (BREAD LOAF) T SPELLS *3ḪT*/AH-KET; (HOUSE) IS THE DETERMINATIVE SIGN. THE WORD COULD MEAN "HORIZON" AS WELL AS "TOMB".

THE LANGUAGE OF THE ELEMENTS

FLAME *sḏt/sedjet* A folded linen cloth (*s*), combines with a cobra (*ḏ*) and a bread loaf (*t*) to spell *sḏt*. The sign of the brazier is a determinative.

RIVER *itrw/eetroo* A reed (*i*), a bread loaf (*t*), a mouth (*r*) and a quail chick (*w*) combine in the word for "river", which is determined by the water ripple sign repeated three times.

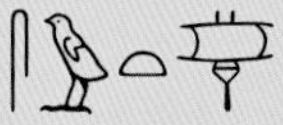

BREEZE *swt/soot* A folded linen cloth (*s*), quail chick (*w*) and a bread loaf (*t*) spell *swt*, with the boat sail symbol (see also main text above) used as a determinative.

RAIN STORM *snm(w)/senmoo* A bolt, a water ripple, a sign that possibly represents a butcher's knife and an owl appear in this word; the animal with forked tail is probably related to the god of disorder, Seth. The word is determined by the image of a sky with sheeting rain.

SEA *w3ḏ-wr/ wadge wier* The sign furthest left – a papyrus with a cobra – is an example of a triliteral sign (see pages 22–23) and spells *w3ḏ*. It combines with a sparrow and a mouth; the determinative is a water channel.

LIFE ON EARTH

Over the doorways of their houses some Egyptians painted hieroglyphic inscriptions to attract good fortune to the household. In temples, hieroglyphs were ritually activated to bring divine blessing on the land; in tombs, inscriptions protected the deceased in the underworld. Hieroglyphs brought their magical power to bear in every aspect of Egyptian life and death.

DWELLINGS OF MEN AND GODS

Ancient Egyptian houses were designed to be cool in summer and warm in winter. They were built of mud bricks that had been set in rectangular wooden moulds and dried in the sun; many modern Egyptian houses are made in the same way. Bricks for royal buildings were often stamped with the name of the king.

The sign for "house" *pr/pair* was used as a determinative in words associated with enclosed areas – for example, in *hnw/hen-oo*, "interior". The same house sign also featured in the words for "treasury" *pr-ḥḏ/pair hedge* and "estate" *pr ḏt/pair jet*.

The typical Egyptian house was situated on a common walkway that joined it to other dwellings. Within, rooms opened from a passageway that people entered from the street. The average house consisted of four to six rooms, and many houses had a cellar. Some houses had a flat roof so that people could sleep outside during the summer.

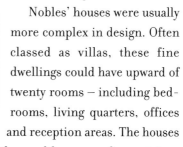

Nobles' houses were usually more complex in design. Often classed as villas, these fine dwellings could have upward of twenty rooms – including bedrooms, living quarters, offices and reception areas. The houses of the wealthy were often set in a walled courtyard that also contained servants' quarters, stables and granaries.

The *pr* sign was also used in the words for people who worked in the home. The word *ḥry pr/herry pair* is often translated "servant" or "house

The pyramids of (left to right) Menkaure, Khepren and Khufu at Giza, modern Cairo, were erected as royal tombs in the Old Kingdom (2625–2130BCE). They were built from limestone with inner chambers of granite that had been transported 600 miles (966 km) from Aswan. Originally all three were covered in fine white Tura limestone casing, some of which remains at the peak of Khepren's pyramid.

DETAIL, CENTRE The scribe Nakht's house *(see pages 46–47)* *has twin roof vents.*

servant" – one who is in the house (see box, page 118); the word for "woman" or "wife" was sometimes written *nbt-pr/nebet-pair* – and then is usually translated "mistress of the house".

The hieroglyphic words for buildings other than houses often used the *pr* sign alongside other signs that indicated the type of building it was. For example, one version of the word for "temple" *ḥwt-nṯr/hewit-netcher* combines with the signs for the temple flagpole and the sacred enclosure. Temples built in honour of the gods were designed to echo the shape of the universe at its first moment of creation – when the primeval mound emerged from the waters of chaos (see page 41). Over years the shape of the mound was gradually incorporated into temple design in that the inner sanctuary – where the statues of the gods were kept and where the divine force was believed to reside – was built on a higher level than the surrounding outer areas of the temple. A distinct form of temple was the royal mortuary temple, built on the king's order as the home for his cult after his death. Typically, these temples were large complexes equipped with a palace, storehouses and a granary. The word for "tomb

BUILDINGS AND BUILDERS

TO BUILD *kd/ked* A building instrument, a hand, a pot and male figure building an enclosure are represented in the verb "to build".

TEMPLE *ḥwt-ꜥ3t/hewit-ahrt* The word for "temple" is often spelled with the temple sign (left), the bread loaf and the enclosure sign.

MONUMENT *mnw/menoo* Scholars have established that the image of a board for a game similar to checkers had the phonetic value *mn*; the pot or bowl repeated three times underneath represented the sound *nw*; together they spell *mnw* in the word for "monument".

OFFICE or HALL *ḫ3/har* The lotus stalk sign spells *ḫ3*, while the vulture reinforces the *3* sound. The image of a hall of columns is the determinative. In some words, the hall symbol stood for the sound *ḫ3*.

A vignette from the Book of the Dead that belonged c.1300BCE to the royal scribe and military officer Nakht shows Nakht and his wife Tjuiu in the garden of their house worshipping Osiris (seated) and Maat (standing). Between the worshippers and deities lies a pool surrounded by trees. Above Nakht's hands is written (in hieratic) his name and above his left hand the phrase "royal scribe".

chamber" *is/ees* used the symbols of a flowering reed, a bundle of reeds, a bolt and the *pr* house sign determinative.

The *pr* sign was also used in *mnw/menoo*, "fortress". Forts were built on the southern and northern frontiers of Egypt, and were often simple buildings used as look-out posts, supply stations and policing points from which river traffic and foreign migration could be controlled. In the Middle and New Kingdoms (1980–1075BCE), forts were built on a larger scale, complete with temples, barracks and official quarters. Buhen fort, about 156 miles (250km) upstream from Aswan in Lower Nubia, was equipped with a drawbridge and protected by walls 13ft (4m) thick in the Twelfth Dynasty (1938–1759BCE).

THE HARVEST OF THE FIELDS

This image of the grape harvest is from the tomb of Nakht, a scribe and astronomer under Tuthmosis IV (c.1400–1390BCE). The first man picks the grapes and his companion carries a full basket as well as a grape cluster.

PAGES 48–49 *At Beni Hasan in Upper Egypt, the lush Nile floodplain stands out in striking contrast to the arid desert.*

The Greek historian Herodotus, writing in the fifth century BCE, described Egypt as a rich and fertile land casually tended by idle farmers. But the truth was very different – both in Herodotus's era and centuries earlier. Ancient Egyptian farmers were taxed on their land, and when crops were poor – due to unfavourable weather or attacks by insects or rodents – the farmers were exploited or beaten by tax collectors, who had the power to imprison or sell into slavery members of farmers' families. The *Satire of the Trades*, an ancient Egyptian instruction text, declares that farmers worked so hard that their fingers were swollen and stinking – and lived such a hard, miserable life that they wailed "more than a guinea fowl" and cried "louder than a raven".

Ancient Egyptian farmers used lightweight wooden ploughs pulled by cattle. Two men usually drove each team: while one stayed at the handles and controlled the plough, the other guided the animals. Pictorial images of agricultural tools and produce were used in words connected to farming. The sickle and the hoe were employed in the words for " to reap"

COUNTRY LIFE

FIELD *3ḥt/ahht* The sign for a vulture (*3*) was often used in words describing or connected to open country and the activities of the fields. Here it combines with the signs of a twisted flax (*ḥ*) and a bread loaf (*t*) to spell "field" *3ḥt*. The word is determined by the symbol of an irrigation canal.

TO PLOUGH *sk3/skar* The vulture is repeated from the word for field and combines with the signs of a folded cloth, embracing arms, a plough and a man with a stick.

COUNTRYSIDE *sḫt/seket* A row of cultivated reeds combines with a bread loaf and the irrigation canal sign to spell "countryside"; the word is sometimes considered to be a variant of "field" as written left.

GRANARY *šnwt/shenoot* A loop of rope (*šn*) a water ripple (*n*), a bowl (*nw*), a quail chick (*w*), a bread loaf (*t*) spell *šnwt*, "granary". The word is determined by a symbol that represents a grain heap placed on a raised floor or platform.

3sḫ/ash and "to cultivate" ḥbs/heb-esk. An alternative way of writing "to reap" 3sḫ/ash used a simple knife as determinative and combined it with the signs for vulture, a bolt and a placenta. Similarly, an image of a plough is part of the word for that instrument (see box, left).

Following the plough, a peasant would distribute the seed, which he carried in a basket suspended from his neck. The fertility of the land depended on the River Nile and on human land management. The annual flooding of the Nile, which occurred throughout the summer months, conveyed rich alluvial silt from the central African highlands to the Nile Valley. The river water and its silt was filtered to the fields through manmade irrigation channels. The symbol of an irrigation channel was the determinative sign in the word for "field" (see box, opposite); the word for the "inundation" 3ḫt/akhet combined the vulture,

Details (left, centre and right columns) from the west Theban burial chamber of Sennedjem (c.1290BCE) spell the words below.

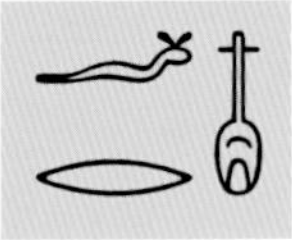

1 HEART AND TRACHEA (RIGHT), MOUTH (LEFT) AND HORNED VIPER (ABOVE) SPELL NFR/NEFER "BEAUTIFUL".

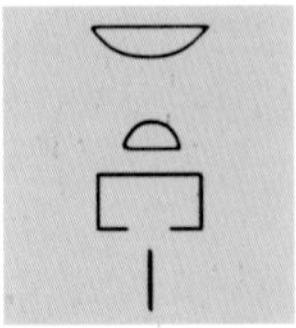

2 DWELLING, WITH BREADLOAF AND BASKET ABOVE, SPELL NBT PR/NEBET PEAR "MISTRESS OF THE HOUSE".

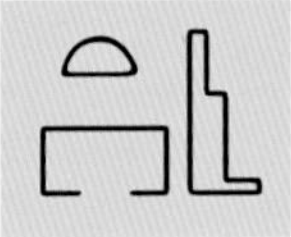

3 THRONE (RIGHT), DWELLING (LEFT, BELOW) AND LOAF (ABOVE) SPELL ST/SET "SEAT OR PLACE".

the image of a pool with lotus flowers, a placenta and a bread loaf sign. The height of the river, measured by means of a device called a Nilometer, determined whether a harvest would be successful or not. Nilometers, one of which was built at the site of modern Aswan, consisted of steps against which the river's height was measured. If the river was low, the land was starved of essential nutrients, and the people were threatened with famine.

The crops were fully grown and harvested before the following year's inundation. The cereal crops were taken to the nearest village and stored in large baskets. Forks were used to thresh the wheat, while animals trampled the grain. After winnowing, the produce was stored in a granary that was often situated in the temple precinct; here, the harvest was measured and recorded by the scribes.

A pictorial sign that incorporates the image of a grain cask was used in the word for a measurement known to the ancient Egyptians as *ḥk3t/hekat*. It also appeared in the word for "barley" *it/eet*. The image of an ear of wheat was used in the word for "emmer wheat" *bdt/bedet*. Bread was made from cereal grain and baked in large open ovens. Beer was made from fermented barley and sweetened with honey.

1 Beautiful **2 Mistress of the house** **3 Seat or place**

EATING AND DRINKING

The wealthy élite in ancient Egypt enjoyed fine and varied food. They ate a range of meats, including beef, mutton, pork and goat as well as wild fowl, some fish and plenty of fruit and vegetables. The poor, on the other hand, had a basic diet of bread and vegetables such as onions, leeks, lettuce and cucumber, supplemented by fish, animals or birds they caught while hunting.

Hieroglyphic signs relating to eating and drinking were often determined by the figure of a man with hand to mouth. The word for "eat" 𓃹𓈖𓅓𓀁 *wnm/whenem* uses the kneeling figure with hand to mouth alongside a flower (*wn*), a water ripple (*n*) and an owl (*m*). Likewise the word for "hunger" 𓎛𓈎𓂋𓀁 *ḥkr/hek-her* uses the kneeling male figure alongside a twisted flax (*ḥ*), a hill sign (*k*) and a mouth (*r*). Words for meats were often determined by the flesh sign 𓏭 (see box, page 54). The verb "to taste" 𓊪𓂋𓀁 *dp/dep* was determined by both the sign of a bovine tongue 𓄓 and the kneeling man.

Beer was by far the most common drink in ancient Egypt, but by the New Kingdom (1539–1075BCE) the trade and export of wine was also well established. The upper classes served large quantities of both wine and beer at their banquets; the poor drank no wine, but enjoyed beer, which was often flavoured with honey. A honey pot was the determinative in the word for "honey" 𓆤𓏏𓏌 *bjt/beet*, which also used the images of a bee and a bread loaf. The ancient Egyptians were experienced bee-keepers – tending bees in pottery hives in their gardens. Honey and carob seeds were used to sweeten cakes as well as beer.

Images of the pots used to store beer and wine were used in hieroglyhic words

Duck – eaten here by one of Queen Nefertiti's daughters in a partly carved relief decoration at el-Amarna – was enjoyed by the wealthy in ancient Egypt. They also ate pigeon, geese, cranes and quails.

for these drinks. "Beer" *ḥnkt/hen-ket* was determined by an image of a beer jar. A similar jug determinative was used with other liquids. The word for "milk", *irtt/ireet*, combined a reed, an eye with pupil, two bread loaves and a milk jug with plural strokes. Some food or drink words were determined by agricultural symbols such as the earth sign or by bread loaves.

Food was needed for the dead as well as for the living. A continuous supply was required within temples and tombs as offerings to the gods and to the dead. Remains of food have been found in upper-class New Kingdom burials, where funerary meals were stored in pottery jars. People arranged for priests to leave these offerings, and made doubly sure that their souls would be well supplied by commissioning artists to paint food on the walls of the tombs. Most ancient Egyptian tomb scenes represent the deceased at a table piled high with food.

Tomb decorations also show the Egyptians forcefeeding their animals and birds to fatten them up for slaughter. Some reveal butchering techniques, showing cattle bound and garrotted. Four or more men would be required to carry out this procedure. They would bind the left foreleg of the animal and secure it with a slipknot, while the other end of the rope was passed over its shoulders. The animal would then be dragged to the ground. The hind legs and the roped foreleg were tied together, and the butcher cut the beast's throat with a knife. Its blood was drained into a vessel that may have had ritual or religious significance.

FOOD AND DRINK

FOOD *šbw/sheboo* A pool of water (*š*), a foot and leg (*b*), a quail chick (*w*) and a land sign with strokes spells out "food".

TO DRINK *sw(r)i/swer-ee* A folded linen cloth, a sparrow, a mouth sign, a reed and three ripples of water appear in the word for "drink". The determinative, as with many food and drink words (see page 53), is the image of a kneeling man with his hand to his mouth.

MEAT *wʿbt/webet* A water pot on a human leg, a bread loaf and a flesh sign together write *wʿbt* "meat".

BREAD *t/t* Two bread loaves – the flat loaf widely used to represent the sound *t* and a conical one – combine with an earth sign to spell "bread".

A funerary stone slab (c.945–715BCE) shows food offerings to the sun god (left). Details from the inscription's two left columns read "Re-Horakhty-Atum. lord of the two lands".

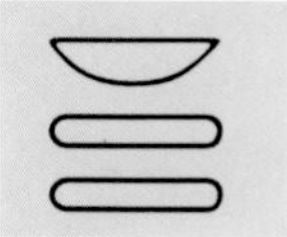

A basket sign (above) nb/neb "lord" combines with horizontal earth signs (below) t3wy/taw(y) "two lands" to spell the title "lord (of the) two lands".

The falcon with the sun symbol and the two lands spells Rʿ-ḥr-3ḫty/Re-Horakhty. The bread loaf sign above a sledge spells tm/Atum.

RECREATION AND SPORT

Female musicians and dancers entertain banquet guests in a wall painting from the Theban tomb of Nebamun, a scribe in the reign of Amenhotep III (c.1390–1353BCE). Details from the inscription in the lower part are explained in the captions opposite.

In ancient Egypt giving a banquet was an important way of enhancing one's social position – as today, entertaining was used for "networking" by officials and dignitaries. Egyptian banquets are portrayed in several tombs of the New Kingdom (1539–1075BCE): servants offer food, drink and floral wreaths to guests, who are dressed in fine linen, wigs and jewelry; musicians perform on oboes, flutes, tambourines and other instruments while entertainers tell stories.

Figurative images are used in many words associated with recreation. The figure of a man placing his hand to his mouth is used both in *ibi/ibbi* "to be thirsty" and *swri/swerry* "to drink", while the image of a beer jar is used in the word for "drunkenness" *th/t-hek*. A dancing man determines the verb *hb/heb* "to dance".

Both men and women enjoyed dancing and acrobatics. In temple and tomb art they are shown performing gymnastic

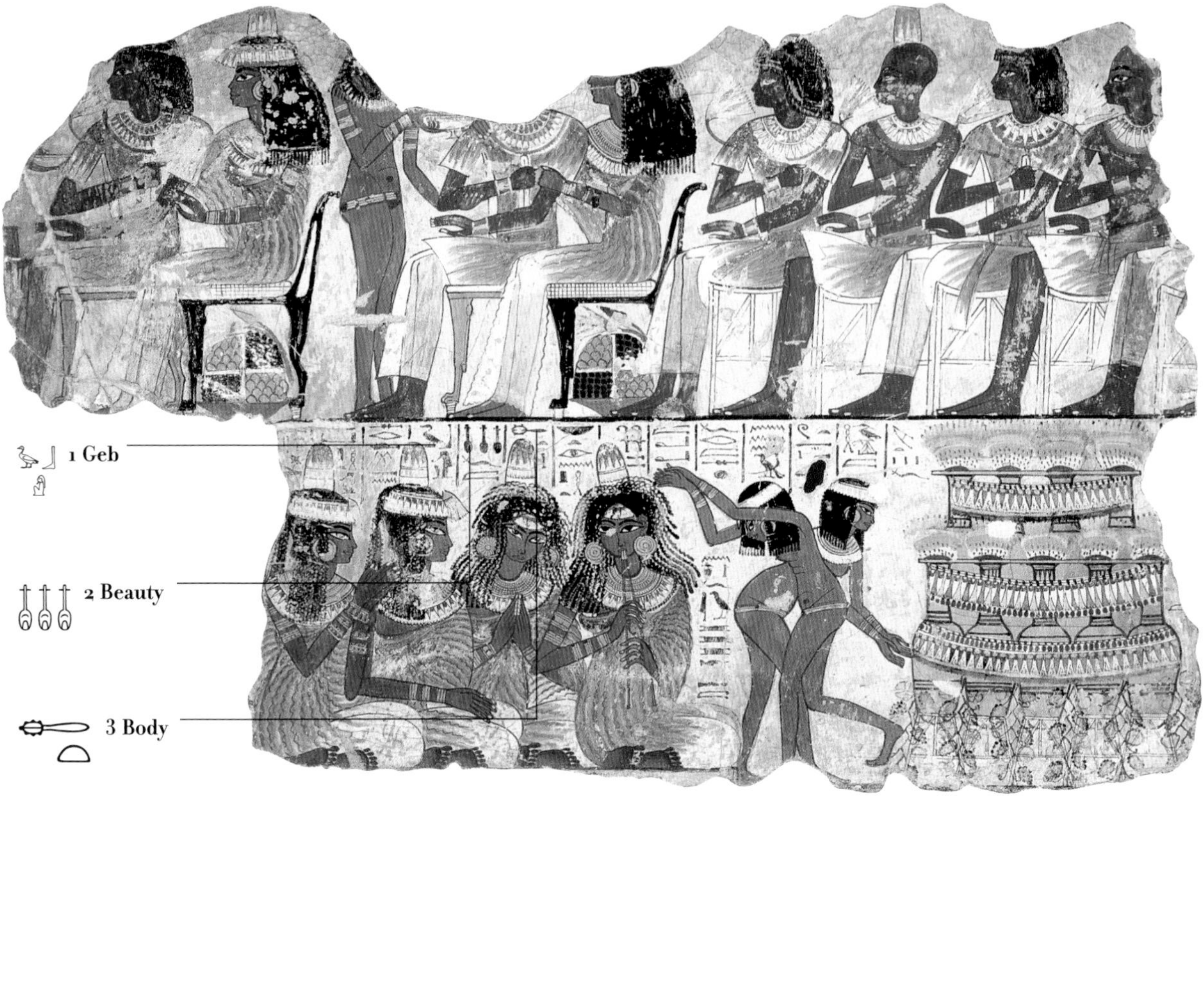

1 Geb

2 Beauty

3 Body

PLEASURABLE PASTIMES

PLEASURE *sḫmḫ-ib/shema-ibb* The final (top) symbol in this word is a heart (*ib*) – the word can also be translated as "distraction of the heart".

BOWSTRING *rwd/rood* Mouth (*r*) quail chick (*w*) and hand (*d*) spell *rwd*, which also means "hard" or "vigorous". This word is determined by a bowstring that is shown with two loops at each end. In practice these loops were used to attach the bowstring to the limbs of the bow.

SHOOT *st/set* The verb "to shoot" includes the symbol of an arrow passing through an animal hide or shield.

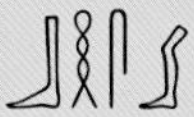

HUNT *bḥs/behes* The verb "to hunt" uses a leg and foot, a flax, a folded cloth and another leg.

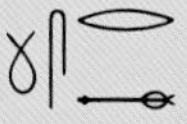

ARROW *šsr/sheser* The arrow that determines this noun is depicted complete with arrowhead and tail feathers.

feats or gyrating to the accompaniment of a small group of musicians.

Sporting exhibitions were part of national life, a common feature of royal celebrations and religious festivals. The king was expected to demonstrate his strength by running a predetermined course as part of his jubilee celebrations. In New Kingdom tombs, temples and funerary monuments, the king was often depicted as an archer and credited with being an accomplished athlete.

Popular sporting recreations included ball games and swimming. Competitions between rope climbers were associated with the festivals of the fertility god Min. Sparring between boat crews and wrestling pairs was also common.

Hunting – especially of lions or wild bulls – was a favourite sport of the upper classes. Representations of hunting on monuments honour victorious military campaigns. The verb "to hunt" (see box, above) could also be written  with an arm determinative or  with the determinative of two walking legs; both are transliterated *bḥs/behes*.

Children's games included a vaulting contest in which two children sat facing each other, their legs and arms extended with their feet touching, while their companions jumped over the outstretched arms which were gradually raised to make it more difficult. Among more restful adult games was Senet, a board game that has often been likened to checkers.

1 The bird or goose (gb) and the leg and foot (another b) spell the name of the earth god Geb. The determinative god figure shows that the word is a divine name.

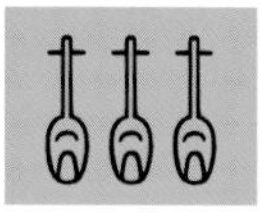

2 Three black sticks with rounded ends represent human hearts attached to the trachea or windpipe. Transliterated nfr(w)/nefer-oo, it is the word for "beauty".

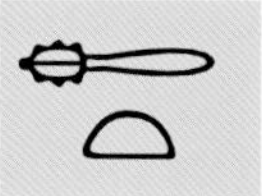

3 "Body" – which is transliterated ẖt – is written with an animal's belly with teats and tail (ẖ) and a bread loaf symbol (t).

CHAPTER THREE

THE SACRED ART OF WRITING

The ancient Egyptians believed that the art of writing and reading hieroglyphs had been revealed by Thoth, god of knowledge and patron deity of scribes. The sacred signs he taught had the power to bring to life the objects they depicted. By painting a word or sentence on a wall, the Egyptians understood that they were creating an animating force that could be harnessed with profitable or disastrous consequences.

Hieroglyphs on this Nineteenth-Dynasty (1292–1190BCE) stele read (top line): "Anubis ... gives water and beer as offerings before this stone block."

THE MAGICAL DIMENSION

In a papyrus of c.1150BCE Ramesses III (c.1187–1156BCE) (right), dressed in royal regalia, faces (from right) Ra-Horakhty, Atum, Iusaaset and Hathor-Nebethepet, deities linked to Heliopolis.

There was little distinction in the ancient Egyptian mind between magic and religion. The divine power embodied by hieroglyphs was used in temple worship to summon the gods, to conduct funerary rites, to sustain the spirit of the deceased after death and to ensure that the dead person was well supplied in the underworld. In day-to-day life religious spells and magic were a powerful means of averting sickness and adversity.

1 A DETAIL FROM THE INSCRIPTION TO THE RIGHT OF HATHOR'S HEAD SHOWS A FALCON WITHIN A DWELLING, ḤT-ḤR/HAT-HOR, THE SIGN OF THE GODDESS.

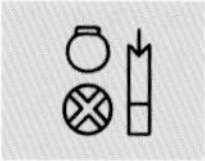

2 IN A DETAIL (BESIDE ATUM) COLUMN AND POT SPELL ꜥIWNW/EEOONEW, THE ANCIENT NAME FOR HELIOPOLIS. THE TOWN SIGN IS THE DETERMINATIVE.

WORSHIP OF THE GODS

The temple was the focus of every ancient Egyptian settlement. In the sacred inner sanctum – where divine power was believed to reside – the high priest of the temple conducted rituals designed to honour the gods and channel their power to the benefit of the land of Egypt. Ultimately the king was the gods' representative on Earth and had to act as an intermediary between gods and people to secure prosperity and fertility for his kingdom. The people understood that the king had passed his ritual duties on to the high priest of each temple.

Every morning in the temple's inner sanctum the high priest greeted the statue of the god in its canopy and worshipped it, offering perfume and incense before anointing the statue with holy oils of cedar and myrrh. He proceeded to adorn the statue with make-up before clothing it and making reverential offerings of food, flowers and drink.

Because the priests made offerings of food to the gods each day, symbols of bread and meat were often used to determine sacred words, For example *sft/sefet*, the word for "anointing oil", combines the signs for a folded linen cloth, a horned snake and an oil jar with the bread loaf sign.

Similarly, because the priests had to keep themselves clean and pure (see pages 112–114), the symbols of a water pot and of flowing water are included in words linked to spiritual cleanliness and purification rituals. *hnw/henoo* the word for "praise" combines the sign for a

OFFERINGS TO SUSTAIN LIFE

The "offering formula" was inscribed on a funerary stele that stood outside the tomb. The spirit of the deceased drew sustenance each time a passer-by read the words of the formula. The offering formula prayer remained essentially unchanged for more than 2,000 years from the early Old Kingdom (2575BCE) onward, and always began with the words "an offering that the king gives", reflecting the belief that the king was the true intemediary between gods and men (see page 60). The following words are part of the offering formula on a stele found in the Middle Kingdom (1980–1630BCE) tomb of the treasurer Tjeti. "An offering that the king gives [and] Osiris, lord of Busiris, foremost of westerners, lord of Abydos, in all his domains. An offering of a thousand of bread and beer, a thousand of ointment jars and clothing, a thousand of everything good and pure ... pure bread of the house of Montu ... libations and food offerings of which spirits love to eat."

1 and 2
3
4

ripple of purifying water with a reed dwelling, a pot and a quail chick. The word is determined by a kneeling man in an act of praise and worship.

The figure of a worshipping male, either raising his arms, kneeling or bowing, is a common determinative in words of worship. Examples include the word for "worship" *sns/seness* (see box). The determinative of "bowing" *ksw/kes-oo* is a bowing man; the other signs are an offering basket and a folded linen cloth. Also *dw3/do-ar*, "adore", depicts a man with arms raised in worship and a five-pointed star.

The power of hieroglyphs resided partly in their mystery – the majority of the population was illiterate. The priests, who were able to read spells and incantations from texts stored in temple libraries, were regarded as having magical powers. The majority of Egyptians had little involvement in temple worship – to seek guidance and reassurance they turned to oracles, who were identified with specific deities. People often built niches in their homes, where they would petition household deities, such as the protector dwarf god Bes or Hathor, goddess of sexuality and childbirth. At large annual festivals the gods normally hidden in sacred inner enclosures were removed from the temple and taken out in public procession.

In an image from the tomb of King Horemheb (c.1319–1292BCE), "words spoken by Osiris, the great god" can be read in the two columns above Osiris's head as detailed below. Horemheb's cartouches (3 and 4) can also be seen.

1 ḎD-MDW/DJED MEDOO "WORDS SPOKEN BY"; ἰN/EEN REITERATES "BY"; WSJR/WESEER OSIRIS.
2 NṮR/NETCHER "GOD"; ˁ3/AH "GREAT" – "WORDS SPOKEN BY OSIRIS, THE GREAT GOD".

WORDS OF PRAISE AND RELIGIOUS RITUAL

WORSHIP *sns/seness* A bolt, a water ripple sign and a folded linen cloth combine in the word for "worship". The word's determinative is the image of a man worshipping with upraised arms.

FESTIVAL *ḥb/heb* A sign often used in words linked to temple ritual is the purification basin, here with a twisted flax and a leg and foot.

TRIBUTE *inw/oo-noo* The word combines an offering pot on walking legs, a water ripple, a pot, a quail chick and a sealed document with three strokes.

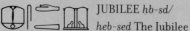

JUBILEE *ḥb-sd/heb-sed* The Jubilee or Sed festival was usually held on the thirtieth anniversary of a king's accession and ritually renewed the monarch's power. The word combines a bowl used in ritual practices, a folded linen cloth, a hand and a strip of land with an image (as determinative) of the hall used during the Sed festival.

THE ART OF MAGIC

To the ancient Egyptians hieroglyphs were magical tools. Hieroglyphic writing was used in administration as well as for sacred inscriptions and in spells, but Egyptians were convinced that magical power was always inherent in the signs. They saw pictures and writing as objects that could be brought to life by magic.

In tombs the written and spoken word was a force for life. The spells and incantations known to scholars as the Pyramid Texts, Coffin Texts and the Book of the Dead (see pages 70–75) were intended to raise magical powers to protect the deceased during his or her journey through the underworld after death.

One way of bringing hieroglyphic scripts to magical life was to read them aloud. Inscriptions on the funerary stele (stone slabs) that were placed within or outside tombs recorded the events and deeds of the deceased person's life and were recited each day by the mortuary priest who conducted the tomb owner's funerary cult (see page 100). This was essential for the survival of the deceased's spirit – in effect, if a person's name was spoken, he or she lived. Because written spells often had to be recited in order to have magical power, many signs relating to magic depict human figures holding a hand to their mouth. For example, "magic" was sometimes written *r/r*, using the sign for the mouth. Another way of writing "magic" was *ḥk3/hekka*, using the image of a kneeling man with hand to mouth as the determinative sign.

The sign of outstretched arms used in this second variant of "magic" represents the spirit of the deceased. Magic was used to pacify ghosts. From the Middle Kingdom period (1980–1630BCE) onward, people hired scribes to write letters to the deceased – promising, for example, to make endowments to the mortuary cult of the deceased if the deceased would protect his surviving family from ghosts or illness or provide messages through dreams. The letters were written on papyrus, or on bowls filled with offerings, and left in the tomb.

Written formulae could be brought to magical life by recitation – the priests posessed the power to activate objects through magic. Beginning in the Middle Kingdom, small mummy-like servant statues or "shabti" were included among burial goods. When they were needed by the deceased, the shabti would be animated by their hieroglyphic inscriptions and they would then serve the dead person by working for him or her, protecting him or her or catering for his or her material needs in the underworld.

The Egyptians wore amulets in the shape of hieroglyphs such as ☥ ꜥnḫ/annk (a symbol that represented life and wholeness) to keep harm and sickness at bay. They also wore small necklaces containing written petitions. In popular magic, objects derived power from the spells written on them. When a person was sick he or she might drink a draught of water that gained healing power from having been poured over an object inscribed with a spell. Sufferers poured this magic water directly on their wounds or had healing spells written on their skin in hieroglyphic signs: the spell was expected to take effect when the sufferer licked the ink off his or her skin.

The name of Ptahmose, vizier under Amenhotep III (c.1390–1353BCE), can be seen on this shabti, left as an offering to Osiris at Abydos.

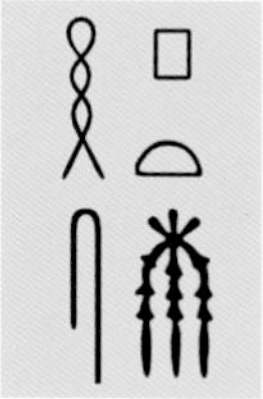

A DETAIL FROM THE SHABTI'S BODY SPELLS THE VIZIER'S NAME IN HIEROGLYPHS: P □ T ⌓ H MS S, PTAHMOSE.

WORDS TO CONJURE WITH

TO INVOKE *nis/niece* The word uses a water ripple, a reed and a folded cloth together with a man with one arm raised in a gesture associated with invocation.

TO CONJURE *šn/shen* The word combines a loop or cord, a water ripple and a kneeling man with hand to mouth.

TO EXORCISE *šnw/shenu* A loop or cord is combined with a water ripple, a coil of rope and a kneeling man shown with his hand to his mouth. The word is also sometimes translated as "conjure".

TOMB INSCRIPTIONS

This relief carving is from the Fourth Dynasty (2625–2500BCE) tomb of Merib at Giza. The inscribed phrase reads "The Royal Acquaintance Merib" as detailed below.

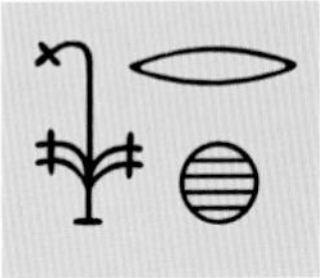

THE SEDGE PLANT MEANS "ROYAL", THE MOUTH AND PLACENTA "ACQUAINTANCE".

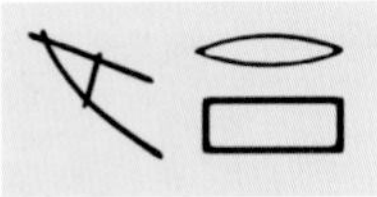

HOE AND MOUTH MAKE MR*i*/MER*i*; THE SQUARE ACTS AS DETERMINATIVE.

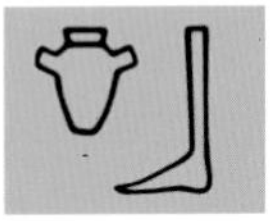

THE HEART IS *i*B/EBB; THE LEG ALSO SPELLS B/B.

A secure tomb was essential to the Egyptian understanding of life after death. The tomb served as a resting place for the deceased and was fitted with all the provisions and equipment necessary for survival in the afterworld. Early tombs were pit graves in the sand, but then many were capped with a stone superstructure later called a mastaba (from the Arabic for "bench"). It was from these humble structures – now known as mastaba tombs – that the pyramid evolved.

During the New Kingdom (1539–1075BCE), Tuthmosis I (*c*.1493–1482BCE), seeking a secure and secret location for his tomb, is believed to have built the first of many sepulchres in the Valley of the Kings, western Thebes. Here royal tombs were hewn from the rock face with simple copper tools. The tombs were inscribed with magical maps intended to guide the newly deceased through the underworld and decorated with scenes and spells from the Book of the Dead (see page 74), as well as royal names and titles.

Only the élite built private tombs. In the Old Kingdom (2625–2130BCE), the tombs of nobles were situated around the

HOUSES OF THE DEAD

TO ROT *hw3/hewa* The word is made up of a twisted flax, a brazier and a vulture and is determined by the symbol of a tumour.

TO EMBALM *sdwḥ/sedooah* The word contains the images of a folded cloth (*s*), a hand (*d*), a quail chick (*w*) and a placenta (*ḥ*). The sign of a tumour and an arm are used as determinatives.

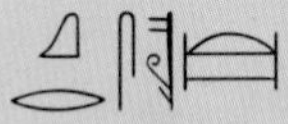

TO BURY *ḳrs/keris* The verb "to bury" is determined by a harpoon head, and the image of a sarcophagus – the stone coffin that contained the Egyptian mummy.

TOMB *3ḫt/ah-het* The word consists of the Sun rising over a mountain horizon and the bread loaf symbol. The house sign is the determinative because the tomb was the "house" of the deceased.

MUMMY *w-j/weee* The sign of an upright body-shaped coffin, complete with the image of a false beard, is used to determine the word "mummy".

great pyramid complexes, so that in death courtiers would be close to their king. Courtiers then began to build tombs in stone carved with exquisite and detailed hieroglyphic inscriptions. The tombs were provided with niches or false doors, where offerings were left for the dead. The deceased's *ka* – his or her life energy, a living "double" created at birth who survived after death – was able to pass through the false door areas and re-enter the world. Rock-cut chambers were added, and the inscriptions in them supply scholars with fascinating details of officials' lives in the Middle Kingdom (1980–1630BCE).

Many private tombs were built at Thebes during the New Kingdom. They were generally T-shaped structures, consisting of a transverse hall that led into a corridor, and their walls were decorated with portraits of the tomb owner and his or her family and scenes of daily life.

Private tombs contained a superstructure that was accessible to the living, and a substructure that contained the body of the deceased; this chamber was sealed at the burial. Funerary goods and personal possessions were buried with the mummy. The family of the deceased would pay for private ceremonies in the outer area of the tomb, where a priest would make offerings and conduct rituals for the dead person.

A standing column (see 9)

A flagpole, associated with temples, and often used in sacred words (see 9)

The sickle sign (see 7)

A basket sign together with a bread sign, "mistress" (see 4)

The eye and pupil, depicted without eyepaint, here part of the name Osiris (see 1)

A human arm and hand (see 9)

A papyrus roll (see 9)

A seated god, wearing the royal or divine beard (see 1)

Two strips of land (see 5)

A sparrow (see 3)

READING A TOMB INSCRIPTION

One of the chief wives of Ramesses II (*c*.1279–1213BCE), Queen Nefertari was buried in the Valley of the Queens at Thebes. The fact that the seated figures in the inscription face rightward indicates that the writing should be read from right to left; as with all hieroglyphic inscriptions, it runs from top to bottom. It reads: "Osiris the Great Royal Wife, Mistress of the Two Lands Nefertari, justified in the presence of Osiris the great god". Nefertari is linked to Osiris because the deceased were believed to be united with that deity – god of the underworld and of resurrection – at death; she is "justified in the presence of Osiris" because, like all souls, she had to be judged by Osiris before proceeding to the afterlife. "Mistress of the Two Lands", a royal epithet, refers to Upper and Lower Egypt. Nefertari wears the vulture headdress of the goddess Mut.

1 "Osiris" *wsir/wisir*: the eye symbol usually means "to do" or "to create"; beneath it are the throne and the seated figure of the god. The combination can be translated "creator of the throne" or "the throne" (see page 89).

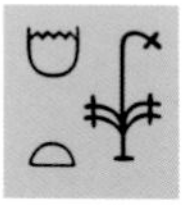

2 "Royal wife" *ḥmt nsw/hemet-nesoo* uses the sedge plant (right) often associated with Upper Egypt and used in titles of rulers of the kingdom. The signs for a well full of water (top left) and the bread loaf, used as a feminine determinative, spell "wife" or "woman".

3 "Great" *wrt/weret* uses the sign of the sparrow with upraised tail that is generally used to denote importance or pre-eminence.

4 "Mistress" *nbt/nebet* has a wickerwork basket (above) that means "lord" – or "mistress" when used with the feminine determinative (*t*).

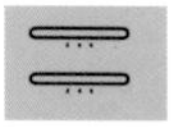

5 The twin horizontals *t3wy/taway* indicate "the Two Lands", Upper and Lower Egypt. "Lord [or mistress] of the Two Lands" was a commonly used royal epithet.

6 The cartouche contains the queen's name and epithet "Nefertari, beloved of Mut" (*nfrt-jry mwt n mrt/nefert ahry moot n meret*). Mut was consort of the god Amun, and mother of the moon god Khonsu.

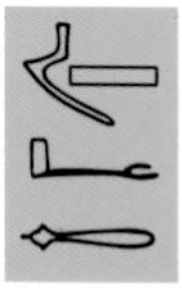

7 "Justified" *m3ʿ-ḫrw/maa herew* is a commonly used honorary epithet. It contains the symbol of the sickle and an unknown sign together with an arm and hand and a wooden column.

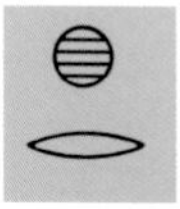

8 "Before" *ḫr/hair* uses the sign of a scored circle, thought to represent a human placenta (*ḫ*) and the sign of the mouth (*r*). Beneath it, at the foot of the third column of the inscription, "Osiris" is repeated (see No. 1, left).

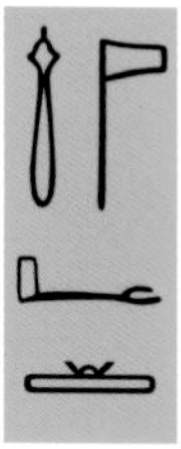

9 "Great god" *nṯr ʿ/netcher-ah* combines the flagpole ("god") with a baton and an arm above a papyrus roll (together spelling "great").

THE PYRAMID TEXTS

The oldest surviving example of Egyptian religious writing, the Pyramid Texts were discovered carved on the walls of the burial chamber in the pyramid of Unas (*c*.2371–2350BCE), the last king of the Fifth Dynasty. They consist of a group of ritualistic utterances designed to protect and rejuvenate the dead king's body in the afterlife, and are divided into five major categories – spells, hymns, litanies, glorifications and incantations. They contain a list of offerings intended to provide the king with all the supplies he would need in the underworld.

The texts suggest that knitting together bones and bodily parts was a prerequisite for the survival and resurrection of the king's body. This is the first reference to the importance of the preservation of the corpse by mummification. The texts also give expression to ancient Egyptian religious doctrine about the origins of life as these doctrines were formulated in Heliopolis: the account casts Atum as the creator deity who gave issue to eight gods and goddesses – Shu, Tefnut, Geb, Nut, Osiris, Seth, Isis and Nepthys (see pages 144–145). The writings also contain the earliest known references to a primordial egg as the source of the first generations of humankind. Other versions of the texts were found in the pyramids of kings Teti, Pepy I, Merenre and Pepy II in the Sixth Dynasty (2350–2170BCE).

IN THE COMPANY OF RE

In the Pyramid Texts, Atum is seen as the primeval procreator god (see main text). The texts deal with the death of the king, and his voyage after death through the sky and the underworld in the company of the sun god Re. In this extract the king ascends in triumph to the celestial realms:

"The sky is overcast,
The stars are darkened,
The celestial expanses quiver,
The planets are still,
For they have seen the king appearing
in power
As a god who lives on his fathers
And feeds on his mothers;
The king's master of wisdom
Whose mother knows not his name.
The glory of the king is in the sky,
His power is in the horizon,
Like Atum, his father who begot him,
And the son is mightier than he."

The interior walls of the pyramid of King Unas (c.2371–2350BCE) are covered with the oldest surviving Pyramid Texts, inscriptions that the king and his subjects believed would guide him to safety in the afterlife. Unas's pyramid was erected near the southwest corner of Djoser's step pyramid at Saqqara.

COFFIN TEXTS

This painted wooden coffin belonged to the nobleman Senbi, who was buried at Meir in Middle Egypt in c.1900BCE. His body was laid on its side so that he could "see out" through the painted eyes that decorate the coffin; his spirit could pass through the "door" beneath to dwell among the living.

During the Middle and New Kingdoms (1980–1075BCE), the spells and other magical writings that had been carved on the walls of pyramids in the Old Kingdom (see pages 70–71) were written on coffin panels, shrouds and papyri. Today we know these Middle and New Kingdom writings as the Coffin Texts and the Book of the Dead (see pages 74–75).

From the Coffin Texts we can see that Egyptians had now begun to believe in an afterlife for all people rather than – as previously – just for the king. The extension of the promise of immortality to social classes other than royalty coincided with a breakdown in central authority and the rise of powerful local rulers.

Life after death was fraught with danger and could be brought to a sudden end. The Coffin Texts often refer to the "second death" – the damnation of the spirit or soul after the "first death" of the body. The second death might occur after the weighing of the heart against the feather of Maat in the Hall of Judgment (see pages 88–89); the soul could be destroyed by a demon called "the devourer".

By the Middle Kingdom ordinary Egyptians had begun to issue direct, personal petitions to the gods, whereas in predynastic and Old Kingdom times they had relied on the king to provide spiritual favours. Increasingly individuals were seen to have equal rights and obligations.

EMPOWERED TO LIVE FOREVER

The spells in the Coffin Texts empowered the deceased to escape negative judgment before Osiris and the "second death" (see main text). They were designed for reciting, as this extract makes clear:

"I am lord of the flame who lives on truth, lord of eternity, maker of joy ... I am he who is in his shrine, master of action who destroys the storm ... Lord of the winds who announces the northwind ... Lord of light, maker of light, who lights the sky with his beauty. I am he in his name! Make way for me, that I may see Nun and Amun! For I am that equipped spirit who passes by the [guards]. They do not speak for fear of Him-whose-name-is-hidden, who is in my body ... any person who knows this spell, he will be like Re in the eastern sky, like Osiris in the netherworld. He will go down to the circle of fire, without the flame touching him ever!"

The Coffin Texts also feature a vision of paradise that corresponded closely with life on Earth. Paradise appeared under names such as the "Field of Reeds" or the "Field of Turquoise", and was imagined in terms of the Egyptian countryside. The spells in the Coffin Texts reveal that eating and drinking, sexual relations, the cultivation of land and the waging of war all continued in the afterlife. Offering formulae (see pages 59 and 64), models and tomb paintings provided the dead with a supply of goods and servants to attend to their needs in the underworld.

THE BOOK OF THE DEAD

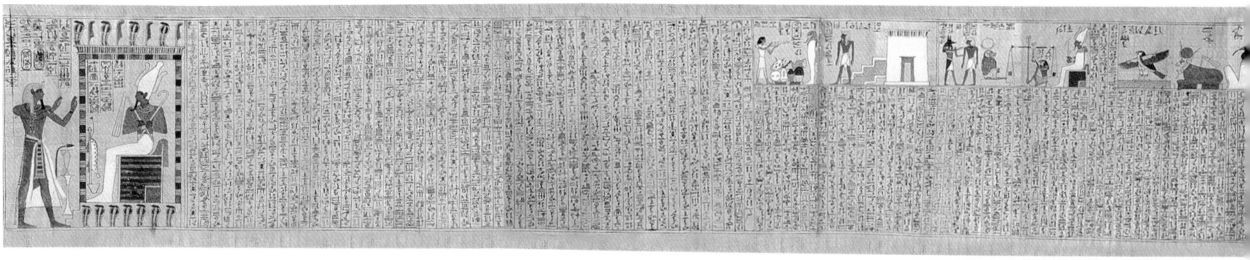

In the Book of the Dead of high priest Pinedjem (c.1065–1045BCE), a detail from above the priest's head (extreme left) reads "Son of Re, of his body, his beloved" (see below).

SPELLS S3-Rʿ/SAR RAY "SON OF RE", N "OF", HT F/HET-EF, "HIS BODY" MRJ/MERRY F/EF "HIS BELOVED", A COMMONLY USED ROYAL EPITHET.

After physical death the ancient Egyptian expected to become one with Osiris. The deceased would travel with Re on a solar boat through the perilous realms of the underworld, a journey littered with obstacles, traps and evil demons that could be negotiated successfully by the recitation of a compilation of spells called the "Spells for Going Forth By Day", now known as the Book of the Dead. Placed on or near the mummy, the Book of the Dead functioned as a map of the underworld and guide to survival there.

From 1506BCE onward, the rulers of Egypt were buried in rock-cut tombs in the Valley of the Kings on the west bank at Thebes. The earliest version of the Book of the Dead was found on royal shrouds and papyri of the seventeenth century BCE. Some of these spells were derived from the Coffin Texts (see pages 72–73), while others were new. Examples of papyri that were inscribed with the Book of the Dead were soon included in the burials of important people unrelated to the royal line. The deceased were often buried with papyri that they had owned and used in life, while a mass production of these papyri meant that the Egyptians could buy a customized version of the script, and simply enter their own names in the appropriate spaces in the text. Illustrations became important in the Book of the Dead, and the images were often transferred to the walls of royal and private tombs.

On his journey to the Field of Reeds (see page 73), the deceased would go through gates guarded by demons. To pass, he would have to stand before these entities and state: "I know you, I know your name", as in these extracts:

"O you gates, O you who keep the gates because of Osiris, O you who guard them and who report the affairs of the Two Lands to Osiris every day: I know you and I know your names." "What is said ... when arriving at the third portal of Osiris:

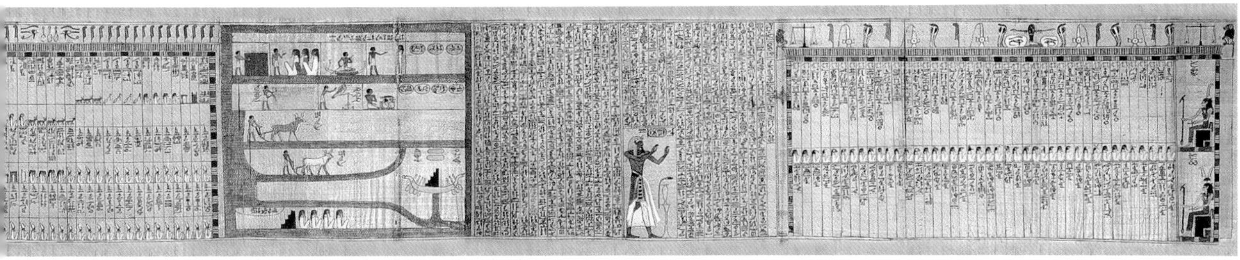

Make a way for me, for I know you ... 'Mistress of altars, great of oblations, who pleases every god therewith on the day of faring upstream to Abydos' is your name. 'He who makes brightness' is the name of her doorkeeper."

Extracts from the Book of the Dead were sometimes used as amulets to protect the living from the dead: fragments of the text were worn by the living, but they have also been found around the necks of mummies. This type of amulet was found around the neck of a high priest of Amun who was buried at Thebes. Spells from the Book of the Dead were also used during the mummification process. The spells describe the correct placement for amulets on the body; some sections of the Book of the Dead were recited as the body was mummified.

A SPELL FOR SENDING A SOUL AND WALKING OUT BY DAY

This spell from the Book of the Dead gave the deceased the power to return to the world of the living.

"In peace, O Anubis! It goes well with the son of Re at peace with my Sacred Eye; may you glorify my soul and my shade that they may see Re ... I ask that I may come and go and that I may have power in my feet so that this person may see him in any place where he is, in my nature, in my wisdom, and in the true shape of my equipped and divine spirit. It shines as Re, it travels as Hathor. Therefore you have granted that my soul and my shade may walk on their feet to the place where this person is, so that he may stand, sit and walk, and enter into his chapel of eternity, because I am one of the entourage of Osiris ... and no god can be created when I am silent."

HOW TO READ OBJECTS

The ancient Egyptians did not have a word for "art" and the concept of decoration with no practical or magical function would have been foreign to them. But many of their everyday objects were intricately inscribed – and the images and hieroglyphs covering the surface of statues, jewelry or weapons can provide invaluable information about the items' use and ownership.

STATUES

A statue was not just a representation, but also an embodiment of a person and a home for the soul should the mummy be damaged, enabling existence beyond the grave. The Egyptians put statues in tombs and private chapels, and worshipped carved images of gods or kings at cult centres. They considered both kinds of statue to be capable of possessing life, and believed that the statues could be animated by magical ritual. To damage a statue or other image of an individual was a way of harming that person; for example, the Egyptians destroyed the eyes and noses of certain statues in an attempt to wipe out the person's spiritual existence by preventing them breathing "the breath of life". The word 𓏏𓅱𓏏𓀾 *twt/tut* was often

THE BODY LANGUAGE OF STATUES

The style and placement of a statue helped the illiterate to decipher its meaning. Royal statues outside the temple gateway identified the king as divine protector, while the statue's dress and regalia indicated the king's religious or mythical associations. Standing figures with their feet together echo the mummiform pose, indicating mortality. Striding statues show the king's virile nature, and can be likened to 𓂻 or 𓂽, a hieroglyphic ideogram for action. A seated king is often shown on a throne, a sign used in the name for Isis, 𓊨𓏏𓁐 *3st/Ah-set*. The throne is an emblem of the king's throne – his divine seat.

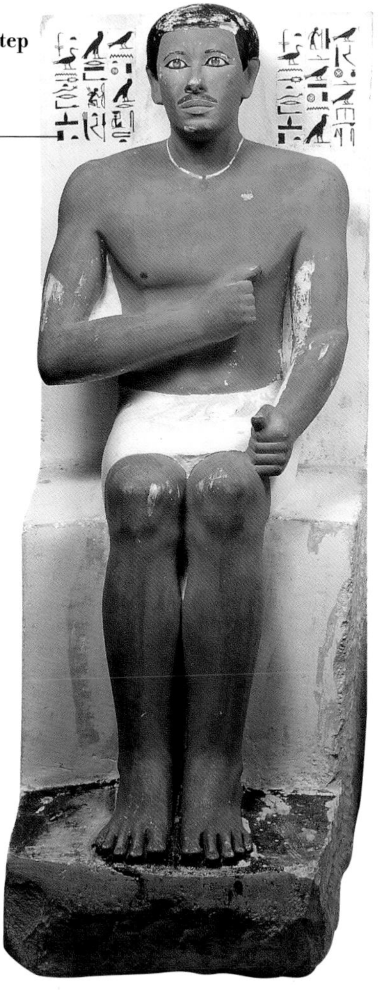

These life sized painted limestone statues of Prince Rahotep and his wife Nofret are from the couple's mastaba tomb at Meidum. They are dated to the reign of King Sneferu (c.2625–2585BCE). Statues of women were often painted to indicate a lighter skin colouring than that of men.

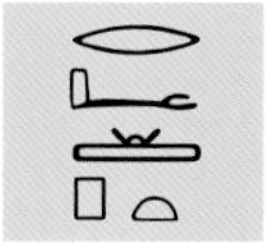

1 (MOUTH, R/RAR) (ARM, ʿ/ AH) (PAPYRUS ROLL, ḤTP/HETEP), (BREAD LOAF T/T), (STOOL, P/P) COMBINE TO SPELL RḤTP/RAHOTEP.

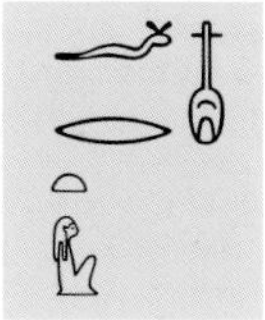

2 (NFR/NEFER) (F/F) (R/R) (T/T) SPELL NFRT/NOFRET. THE SEATED FIGURE IS THE FEMALE DETERMINATIVE.

used to mean "statue", while Tut-ankh described the living image – a term reiterated in the name of Tutankhamun (*c*.1332–1322BCE) ("living image of Amun").

Hieroglyphs often appear on the back pillars, bases, aprons and kilts of statues. The *ka* sign above a statue's head indicates that it was made for a tomb. Block statues sometimes included a front panel of autobiographical text, but sculptors generally communicated with the masses in other ways. Many statues were carved with the recognizable features or characteristics of rulers. Symbols such as the lapwing or a man depicted raising his hands may have been written on the base of statues or monuments to direct citizens to public areas in temples.

JEWELRY

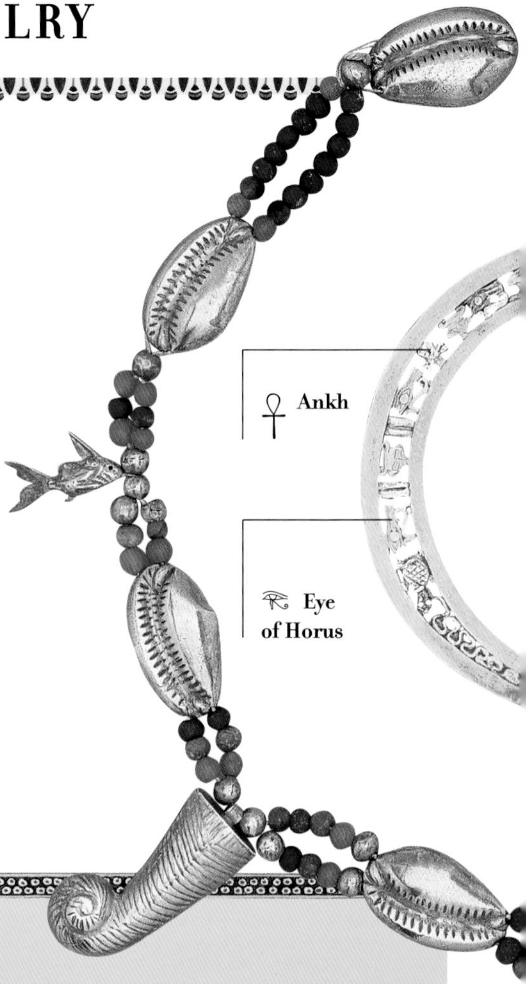

Both men and women wore jewelry in ancient Egypt. Soldiers wore necklaces awarded in honour of military achievement, while the rich used jewelry as a symbol of rank. People of all classes wore amulets inscribed with auspicious phrases or symbols that had positive associations; they believed that these gave the amulets potent magical powers to avert harm. Signs inscribed on amulets included the eye of Horus 𓂀 *wḏ3t/wedjat*, which represented healing (see page 65), the ankh symbol ☥ *ꜥnḫ/annk* and the falcon sign 𓅃 *ḥrw/heroo* that represented the god Horus.

The placement of amulets was an important part of the mummification process. The Egyptians placed necklaces,

PERSONAL ADORNMENT

AMULET *s3/sar* Thought to represent a papyrus shelter, the *s3* sign was a symbol of protection. As well as being used as the word for "amulet", the sign was often associated with Taweret, the goddess of childbirth.

COLLAR *wsḫ/wesekh* The word includes a quail chick, a folded cloth, a placenta and a collar.

SIGNET RING *ḏbꜥt/debart* The word includes the representation of a finger, a bread loaf and a cylinder seal attached to a bead necklace.

DIADEM *nfr-ḥ3t/nefer-hat* The trachea and lungs (*nfr*) appears with the foreparts of a lion (*ḥ3t*), a sign that means "front" or "foremost". A loaf (*t*) and stroke complete the word.

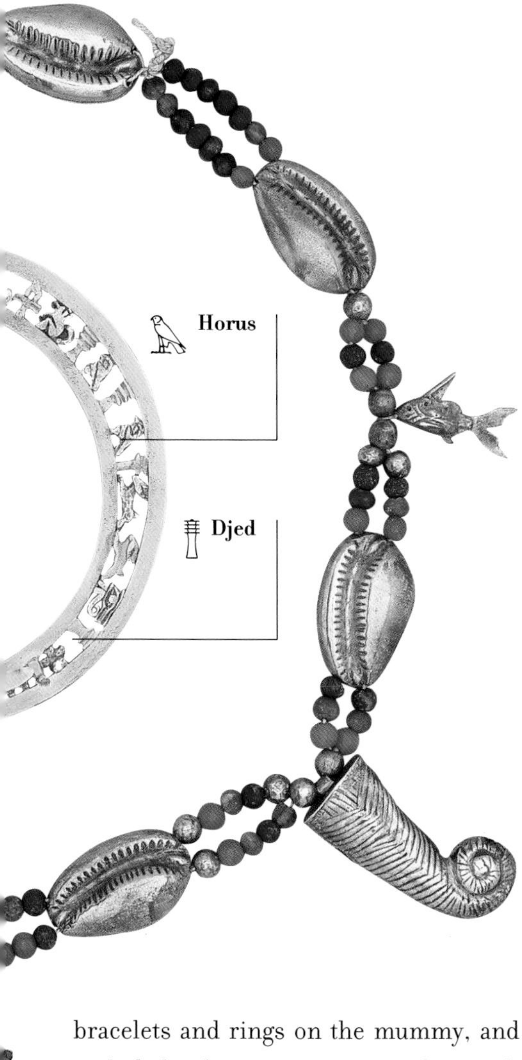

bracelets and rings on the mummy, and included other items among the tomb provisions. Portraits on coffin panels often show the deceased wearing jewelry, while other tomb and temple representations and illustrated papyri show necklaces, earrings and bracelets worn with fine linen garments.

In addition to being used to inscribe amulets, hieroglyphs identified jewelry. Scarab rings were incised with their owner's names and titles, while personal and honorific jewelry belonging to a king often bore his nomen and prenomen (see pages 82–85) – placed in cartouches, panels, clasps and on rings.

Craftsmen laboured in workshops based in temple and palace precincts to produce elaborate jewelry. Egyptologists know little of the jewelrymakers themselves, but illustrations of their techniques can be seen in tombs on the west bank at modern-day Luxor.

The mining and quarrying of precious stones *3t/art* is often described in biographical inscriptions and administrative papyri. The miners worshipped Hathor, known as the "goddess of turquoise" – a stone highly regarded by the ancient Egyptians and represented by the word *mfk3t/mafkat*. Other popular stones included rock crystal, lapis lazuli *ḫsbd/hesbed*, quartz, carnelian, feldspar, bone and shell; while craftsmen making jewelry for the upper classes also used silver *ḥḏ/hedge*, gold *nbw/neboo* and electrum. Gold was especially favoured and was mined in the southern regions. Other jewelry was brought to Egypt from foreign countries as tribute or as spoils of war. It was given as an offering to the gods.

The ornaments on this Twelfth Dynasty (1938–1759BCE) girdle consist of cowrie shells with beard pendants. The gold bangle (same period) has animal amulets including snakes and bats.

THE ANKH MAY REPRESENT A SANDAL STRAP AND WAS USED AS A SYMBOL FOR LIFE FROM PREDYNASTIC TIMES ONWARD. DEITIES ARE OFTEN DEPICTED HOLDING THE ANKH SYMBOL.

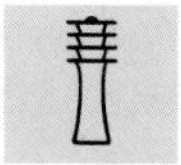

THE DJED COLUMN WAS ASSOCIATED WITH PTAH AND OSIRIS (SEE PAGES 30–33). SOMETIMES IT WAS SHOWN WITH ARMS HOLDING THE CROOK AND FLAIL, EMBLEMS ASSOCIATED WITH OSIRIS AND THE KING.

WEAPONS OF WAR

This ceremonial axehead belonged to the warlike King Ahmose (c.1539–1514BCE), the founder of the Eighteenth Dynasty, who drove the Semitic Hyskos invaders out of Egypt.

In the predynastic period (before 3000BCE), the Egyptians used short bows embellished with horn, but by the Middle Kingdom (1980–1630BCE) archers used a 5ft (1.5m) longbow. New Kingdom (1539–1075BCE) bows were reinforced with sinew, providing greater elasticity and a wider firing range, and arrows – represented in the hieroglyphic word for "arrow" *šsr/shes-er* – were crafted from reed or wood with detachable flint, bone, crystal or copper tips. Archers often carried small bags with spare bowstrings, one of which determines the word for "bowstring" *rwḏ/rood*.

The Egyptian mace had a stone or wooden head fixed to a stave: *ḥḏ/hedge*, the word for "mace", depicts one with a pear-shaped head. Maces were often painted or inscribed. The mace rarely appears in tomb decorations depicting military scenes, but scholars know from other sources that the Egyptians used the instrument to finish off the wounded on the battlefield. Maces were retained as icons in smiting scenes, where they were also shown with crescent blades.

The sword came into use at the start of the Eighteenth Dynasty (1539–1292BCE), when the Egyptians began casting their weapons as single instruments. The word for "sword" *sft/sefet* incorporates the depiction of a blade. The long sword was a thrusting weapon with a pommel grip, while the khepesh was

A SOLDIER'S INSTRUMENTS

AXE *3kḥw/ah-koo* An axe symbol is the determinative sign for this word, which also uses the signs for an Egyptian vulture (*3*), a hillside (*k*), a twisted flax (*ḥ*) and a quail chick (*w*).

DAGGER *m3gsw/ma-gess-oo* A sickle combines with a jar-stand, the plant sign of Upper Egypt, a quail chick and a metal ingot to spell *m3gsw*.

THROWSTICK *ʿmʿ3t/ah-me-aht* The determinative represents a throwstick; the word also uses two arms (*ʿʿ*), an owl (*m*), a vulture (*3*) and a loaf (*t*).

curved, with a sharp outer blade that could behead an enemy with a single stroke. Both were often embellished with fine metalwork and inlays, including the cartouches of kings. Axe blades were cast with hunting motifs or inscribed with cartouches and other hieroglyphs. Perforated copper blades were popular in the Old Kingdom (2625–2130BCE); one of the most powerful weapons of the Middle Kingdom was the crescent-shaped slashing axe. New Kingdom battleaxes had slimmer blades for piercing armour.

Infantrymen were armed with spears or javelins. The "staff" [hieroglyph] *mdw/medoo* was another weapon of the footsoldier, dating back to the predynastic period. It could be be long, short or forked.

A painted wooden casket found in the tomb of Tutankhamun (c.1332–1322BCE) depicts the king triumphing over foreign adversaries, who represent the forces of chaos. Tutankhamun stands in his chariot (centre).

THE POWER OF NAMES

This inscription is part of the "kings' list" carved in the cult temple of Ramesses II (c.1279–1213BCE) at Abydos. Details of the kings' names are examined below.

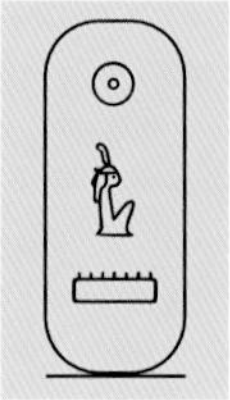

1 King Sety I (*c*.1290–1279BCE): the royal name Mn m3ʿt reʿ/Men-mar-ray, means "enduring of truth is Re".

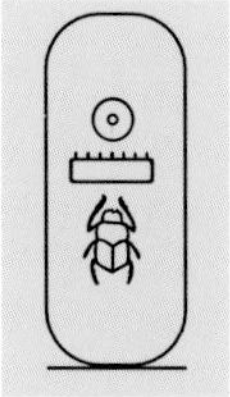

2 King Tuthmosis III (*c*.1479–1425BCE): the name mn ḫpr re/men heper ray means "enduring in appearance is Re".

In the first days, the Egyptians believed, the gods themselves had ruled on Earth. In the creation myths of Heliopolis the falcon god Horus was drawn into conflict with his wicked uncle Seth and had to use all his strength and guile to overthrow his opponent. The first human kings were known as "Followers of Horus" and by the time that Upper and Lower Egypt were united in *c*.3000BCE all Egyptian kings were hailed as "the Living Horus".

THE KING'S TITLES

Identification with Horus established the king as a divinely ordained ruler and a god on Earth. Beginning in the latter part of the Old Kingdom (2625–2130BCE), the king adopted five royal titles.

The first was preceded by the image of Horus *hr* and was known as "the Horus name". The Horus name of Sety I (whose name in the kings' list at Abydos is reproduced, left) was "Strong bull appearing in Thebes", while that of Sesostris I (1919–1875BCE) was "Life of births". The Horus name was sometimes written within a panel representing the king's palace or royal house. In the New Kingdom (1539–1075BCE) "palace" *pr-ʿ3/pair-ah* began to be used as a respectful way of referring to the king and from it by way of the Bible we have derived the word "pharaoh".

The second name was *nbty/nebti* and known as "The Two Ladies". This name placed the king under the protection of the vulture goddess Nekhbet of Upper Egypt and the cobra goddess Wadjet of Lower Egypt. The third name was called "Horus of gold"; the gold may have been intended to refer to the sky drenched in sunlight.

The fourth and fifth names were written or carved within oval loops named cartouches (see page 11). The loops signified the king's universal dominion and magically protected the royal name on monuments. The fourth royal name – known as the prenomen by scholars – was assigned to the king on his accession. It was preceded in inscriptions by *nsw-bit/nesoo beet*. Usually translated as "King

1 King
Sety I
2 King
Tuthmosis III

Please...
no flash inside

of Upper and Lower Egypt", the title also referred to the king's unifying control over other dualities such as desert and cultivated land, human and divine.

The fifth name, called the nomen by scholars, was the king's birth name. The nomen is the name – such as Tuthmosis or Sety – by which modern scholars refer to the king. It is usually preceded by the title "Son of Re" that identifies the monarch as the sun god's heir and representative on Earth. Both the title Son of Re and King of Upper and Lower Egypt were written outside the cartouche.

The king was given other titles, which frequently appear on monuments. These include *nb t3wy/neb-ta-we* "Lord of the Two Lands" and *ntr-nfr/netcher-nefer* "the Good God".

After a king died, the display of his name on monuments guaranteed his eternal survival. It was common practice for monarchs to "usurp" monuments by substituting their own name for the titles of the king who had erected the temple or statue. This brought the usurping king the spiritual benefits associated with the monument. Ramesside kings (c.1292BCE onward) ordered that their names be carved as much as 5 inches (12.5cm) deep to make it harder to erase inscriptions.

Giant seated figures of Ramesses II (1279–1213BCE) guard Abu Simbel temple in Nubia. Cut into sandstone, the statues are 72ft (22m) tall.

THE NOMEN AND PRENOMEN

This table shows the fourth and fifth names of a selection of kings, spanning the Old Kingdom (before the unification of Egypt, when no prenomen was given) to the Greco-Roman period.

SNEFERU
2625–2585BCE

KHUFU
2585–2560BCE

UNAS
2371–2350BCE

MENTUHOTEP
2081–2075BCE

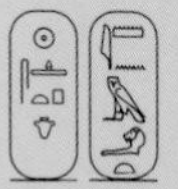
AMENEMHET I
1938–1909BCE

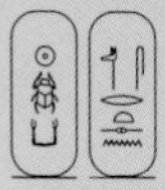
SENWOSRET I
1919–1875BCE

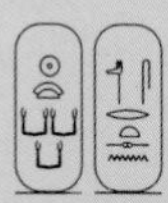
SENWOSRET III
1836–1818BCE

NEFERHOTEP I
1741–1730BCE

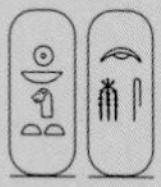
AHMOSE
1539–1514BCE

HATSHEPSUT
1479–1458BCE

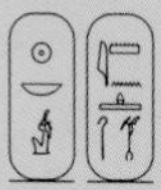
AMENHOTEP III
1390–1353BCE

SETY I
1290–1279BCE

RAMESSES II
1279–1213BCE

RAMESSES IX
1126–1108BCE

SHOSHENQ I
945–924BCE

PTOLEMY I SOTER
305–282BCE

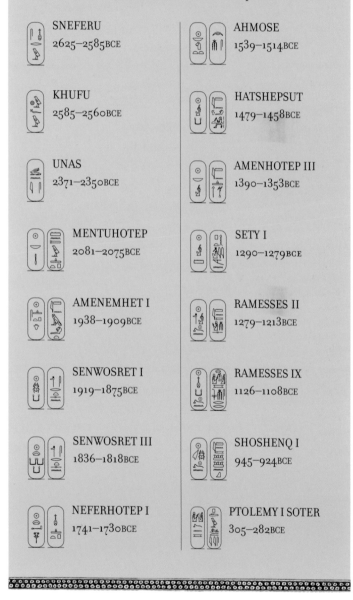

GODS AND GODDESSES

A fragment of painted relief from the tomb of Sety I (c.1290–1279BCE) shows the goddess Maat with her name and title (see below).

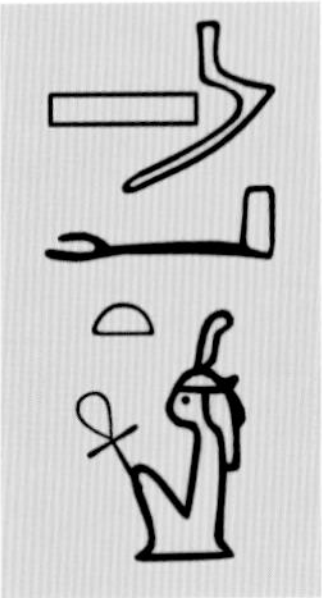

A SICKLE AND AN UNKNOWN SIGN, A FOREARM AND A BREAD SYMBOL SPELL M3ꜥT "TRUTH", MAAT'S EPITHET. THE GODDESS SIGN IS THE DETERMINATIVE.

THE SIGNS FOR THE GOOSE AND THE BREAD LOAF READ S3.T AND THE SUN SYMBOL READS Rꜥ, SPELLING S3.T Rꜥ/SART RAY, THE TITLE "DAUGHTER OF RE".

The Egyptians saw their gods as being governed by the same natural laws as humankind – they carried out human practices, engaged in warfare, and were subject to emotions, illness and death. According to the creation myths as told at Heliopolis in Lower Egypt, the creator deity *ꜥItm/Atum* was father and mother of the gods. In tomb paintings and other representations, Atum was often shown as a human wearing the crowns of Upper and Lower Egypt. Pharaohs were keen to establish divine sanction for their rule by associating themselves with the gods. The most common form of the name of the goddess *3st/Isis* contains the image of a throne. Isis raised her son Horus to defeat his wicked uncle Seth and regain the throne that Seth had stolen from Horus's father Osiris, the first king on Earth; ruling pharaohs were seen as an embodiment of Horus, and Isis was understood to be the mother of the pharaoh. Royal epithets included a "Horus name".

Maat, the goddess of truth and justice, personified order and harmony in the universe. It was the pharaoh's divinely ordained task to re-establish the universal order that had prevailed at the beginning of the world; he is often shown offering to the gods an image of Maat wearing her symbol of an ostrich feather. After death when the soul faced judgment by Osiris, the heart of the deceased person was weighed against the feather of Maat, representing truth (see page 88).

Thoth, a god of wisdom often depicted in scenes of the weighing of the heart, was responsible for calculation in the underworld and one of his tasks was to record the names of the dead. He was believed to have given the Egyptians the key to writing and reading hieroglyphs; scribes were often addressed as the "followers of Thoth". Thoth was occasionally associated with the moon and linked to the ibis (see page 89); he was also often shown in the form of a baboon – an animal that produces piercing shrieks just before dawn and so was connected in the popular imagination to the transition between night and day.

The hieroglyphic names of many deities contain symbols of animals or birds. Horus was widely represented as a falcon, with his wings as the sky and his eyes the sun and the moon. The sign for Horus was sometimes simply a falcon, but could also be a falcon on a standard, as in

In this funerary text of c.1285BCE, the deceased, Hunefer, is led by Anubis to the scales, where his heart is weighed to see if he is worthy to proceed to paradise. Thoth (standing, facing left) notes the positive result; Horus then leads Hunefer forward to meet Osiris (enthroned).

ḥr/heroo, or a falcon on a symbol of gold, as in *ḥr-n-nbw/heroo-n-neboo*. Khnum, a potter god said to have created humans from clay on his wheel, was associated with the flooding of the Nile and known as "lord of the crocodiles", while as a fertility god he was linked to the ram; his name was determined by a god figure whose head has been replaced with that of a ram: *ẖnmw/henmoo*. Anubis, god of embalming, was usually shown as a jackal and one form of his name shows a jackal crouched on a plinth .

The name of one god, however, was often written without using pictorial images. In the creation mythology of Thebes, capital of Upper Egypt, the god Amun was the supreme creator. Known as the "hidden one", he existed beyond the natural world and was concealed even from the other gods. His name was sometimes written using only the phonetic signs that spelled it out, leaving the essence of the god's name unrevealed (see box).

The word for "god" contains the sign of the flagpole: *nṯr/netcher*. The sign shows a cloth attached to a stave, a banner associated with sacred enclosures. The flagpole symbol is also used in the adjective "divine" *nṯr/ netcher* and as a determinative for a god's name. In addition, the flagpole can denote a sacred area, as in *ẖr(t)-nṯr/hurt-netcher*, "necropolis".

A detail from the Hunefer scene shows Horus wearing the sun disc and royal uraeus (crown with cobra motif) in his aspect as "Re-Horakhty – Horus of the Horizon".

THE HOLY ONES OF EGYPT

THOTH A god of wisdom, also known as "Djehuty". His name often contains an image of the ibis, a bird whose curved beak bears a resemblance to the crescent moon. It can also be written with the sign of a bird perched on a sacred standard.

ATUM The sun god and original creator deity whose name means "totality" or "whole".

OSIRIS Funerary and fertility god, brother and husband of Isis. His name includes the sign of the eye and the throne and may mean "he who makes or occupies the throne" or "he who copulates with Isis".

HORUS Son of Isis and Osiris who had to fight Seth for divine kingship. Always shown as a falcon. His name often appears within a rectangular border called a "serekh" that was used in the same way as a cartouche (see page 11).

AMUN His name, "the hidden one" (see main text, left), is written with phonetic signs (*imn*) only.

SETH God of chaos, winds and storm, he is usually shown with a beak, horns and forked tail – the features of an unidentified animal. His birthday was an unlucky day.

NUT Sky goddess, mother of the sun god Re, to whom she gives birth each dawn. Her name depicts a pot placed above the symbol of the sky and includes the bread loaf symbol.

KHNUM Creator god usually shown as a man with a ram's head. The ram was sacred to Khnum.

GEB Earth god, brother and consort to the sky goddess Nut. His body is usually shown green to highlight his connection to vegetation.

ISIS Mistress of magic, consort of Osiris and mother of Horus. The Egyptians believed Isis to be the mother of the ruling pharaoh.

ANUBIS God of embalming, associated with the jackal and often shown as a black, dog-like figure. In ancient Egypt graves were frequently desecrated by packs of scavenger dogs.

KHEPRI A sun god, represented as a scarab beetle. The scarab's young emerge from holes in the ground and the beetle was associated with myths of self-creation and with the emergence of the sun from the underworld at dawn. The same dung beetle symbol was used to mean "to come into existence".

READING A TEMPLE INSCRIPTION

Ramesses II (1279–1213BCE) built a temple at Abu Simbel, on the River Nile south of modern Aswan, in honour of the goddess Hathor and one of his chief wives, Nefertari. The temple stands close to a larger one that the same king built in honour of Amun Re, Ptah and Re-Horakhty. The 35ft (10.5m) statues that flank the entrance to Nefertari's temple represent the king. The inscription on the column at left reads "King of Upper and Lower Egypt, [strong in Truth is Re, Chosen of Re], Son of Re, [Beloved of Amun, Ramesses] ruler of the two lands, the beloved, given life, like Re, forever" as detailed below. The words in brackets are the king's prenomen and nomen (see pages 82–85). The second cartouche is not reproduced because it is damaged, but scholars have reconstructed its probable reading: "Ramesses, Beloved of Amun".

1 "Ruler of Upper and Lower Egypt" – the *nsw-bit/nesoo-beet* sign combines the bee, emblem of Lower Egypt, and the sedge plant, emblem of Upper Egypt. The title was used from *c.*3100BCE onward.

2 "Strong in truth is Re, chosen of Re". Within the royal cartouche the sun sign, the dog's head on a standard, the sign of the goddess Maat, another sun, an agricultural sign and the water ripple combine to spell out one of King Ramesses's five names.

3 "Son of Re" – duck and sun make *s3-rꜥ/sar-ray*. Beneath is the damaged cartouche that reads "Beloved of Amun, Ramesses".

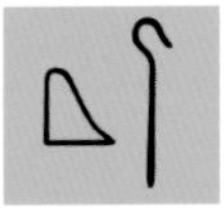

4 "Ruler" *ḥḳ3/hekka* combines the crook sign *ḥḳ3* and a sloping hill. The crook symbol is thought to represent a shepherd's staff.

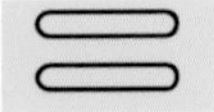

5 "[of] the Two Lands" – the two strips of land *t3wy/tarway* represent the two lands of Upper (southern) and Lower (northern) Egypt also referred to at No. 1, above.

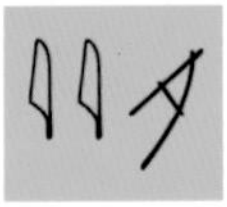

6 "The beloved" *mri/merry* combines the symbols for the hoe and two flowering reeds to spell this royal epithet.

7 "Given" *di/dee* is written with the symbol of a triangular loaf of bread. The conical loaf sign is an example of an ideogram (see page 20).

8 "Life" – the *ꜥnḫ/annk* symbol was widely used a symbol for life. The symbol was used in the word for "mirror" *ꜥnḫ/annk* (see page 95).

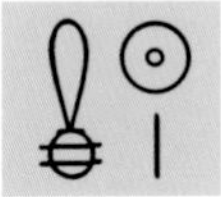

9. "Like Re" is written *rꜥ-mi/ray-mee*, using the symbol of a milk jug in a net together with a sun sign. Ramesses's nomen (in the damaged cartouche) was written *Rꜥ-ms-s/Ramessee* "beloved of Re".

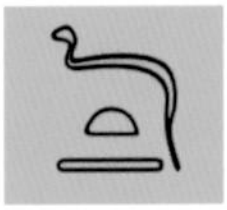

10 "Forever" *ḏt/jet* is written with a cobra, a bread loaf and a strip of land. The same word could be written with two twisted flax signs and a sun sign:

A bee and a sedge plant (see 1)

Ramesses's prenomen (see page 83) within a cartouche (see 2)

A duck and a sun symbol (see 3)

A crook and a sloping hill (see 4)

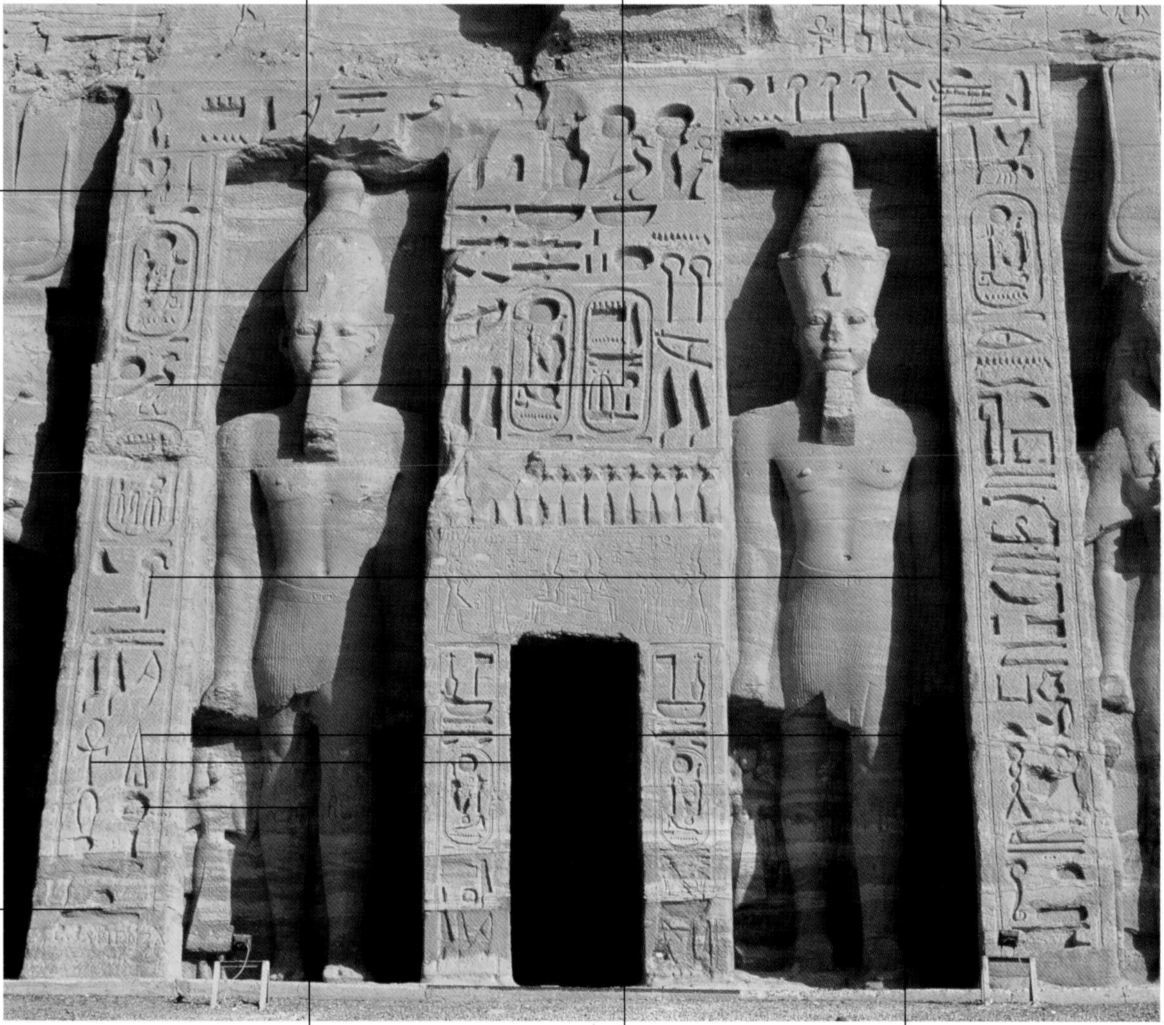

A cobra, a loaf and a land sign (see 10)

A milk jug in a net and a sun symbol (see 9)

The *ankh* symbol (see 8)

A conical loaf (see 7)

CHAPTER FOUR

REALMS OF MEANING

Hieroglyphs illuminate our knowledge of the Egyptian way of life. Our understanding of this ancient people's family life, work, healthcare, state administration, war, worship and correspondence is greatly enhanced by examining hieroglyphic symbols in each sphere.

The eye of Horus is visible on the prow of Amun's barque in this painted scene from the chapel of Sety I (c.1290–1279BCE) at Abydos.

A HEALTHY LIFE

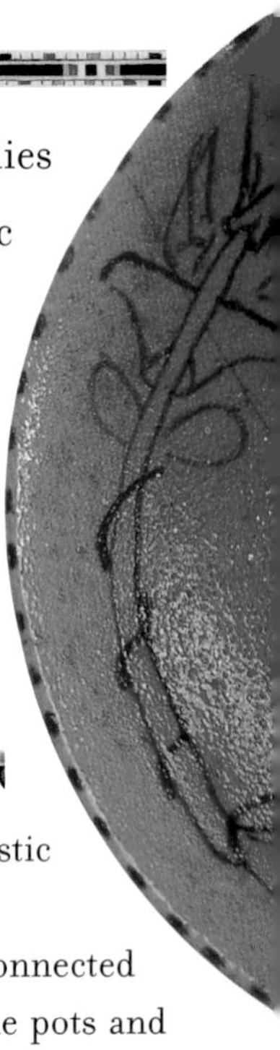

Occasionally Egyptian women were depicted with tattoos, which served both a decorative and a practical purpose. The female musician shown on this blue faience bowl of c.1300BCE has an image of the fertility god Bes tattooed on her upper thigh.

The ancient Egyptians went to great lengths to care for their bodies and enhance their looks, as the many toiletries and cosmetic items found in the tombs of the élite testify. Egyptian doctors had a remarkably detailed knowledge of anatomy; the wide range of treatments – including magic spells and potions – they used to combat illness and disease are documented in medical papyri.

THE BODY BEAUTIFUL

The importance of cleanliness and personal hygiene to the ancient Egyptians is reflected in the large number of hieroglyphic signs that were connected with water and daily washing. Water-pot signs such as and frequently appear in texts about body care.

After washing, wealthy Egyptians rubbed special oils, including sesame oil and moringa oil, onto the skin to moisturize it and help protect it from damage by Egypt's dry climate. They also used resin and oil made from pine kernels to counteract body odour.

Oils such as almond, castor and olive, scented with the essence of herbs and flowers, were employed in the preparation of perfumes. Archeological finds provide evidence for the use of such fragrances from the predynastic period (before 3000BCE).

The most common signs connected with body care represented the pots and jars in which the Egyptians stored the many oils and unguents they used in maintaining personal hygiene. These receptacles took several different forms, the most common being a sealed oil jar , a cup (used as a determinative in *ꜥꜥb/eeeb*, the word for "cup") and a pot *nw/noo*. One of the words for "oil" *mrḥt/mert* combined a hoe (*mr*), a mouth (*r*), a twisted flax (*ḥ*) and a bread loaf (*t*), with an ointment jar used as the determinative sign.

Beauty and body care were closely linked in ancient Egypt – hieroglyphic words relating to both include the sign for

hair 𓈀 *šny/sheny* and various depictions of the eyes, including an eye decorated with paint 𓂀 and an eye with a lower base line 𓁹 . From the dawn of the Egyptian civilization, cosmetics were used to emphasize the eye, which was believed to symbolize life and wholeness. Worn by both men and women, eyepaint also had a practical value – it helped to protect the eyes from the fierce glare of the sun.

Wigs and false braids – made of human hair curled by tongs before being fixed with resin and wax – were widely popular and men and women of all classes wore them. Like eyepaint, wigs may have had a practical as well as an aesthetic purpose: the ancient Egyptians were prone to head-lice, and would often shave their heads in order to prevent lice infestations.

THE ARTS OF BEAUTY

𓄤𓄤𓄤 BEAUTY *nfrw/nefer-oo* Three depictions of the heart and windpipe spell *nfrw*; the verb "to be beautiful" was written 𓄤𓂋 *nfr/nefer*.

𓋴𓏏𓏭 PERFUME/ODOUR *sty/set* A linen cloth, a loaf, two strokes and a tumour sign. The use of the tumour sign in 𓋴𓂧𓅱𓐍 *sdwḫ/ sedoo-ek* "to embalm" may have led to its use here.

𓋹𓈖 MIRROR *ꜥnḫ/annk* The ancient Egyptians associated the reflection in a mirror with the life of the person reflected in it and therefore the hieroglyphic word for "mirror" contains the ankh or symbol of life.

𓂝𓏏 FRAGRANCE *idt/edit* A hand dripping with liquid and a bread loaf make up the word for "fragrance".

THE HEALING ARTS

As a result of their funerary practices , the ancient Egyptians were familiar with the structure of the human skeleton and the organs of the body. They used battle casualties in the study of anatomy, and were knowledgeable about the structure of the skull and treatment of head injuries.

Most of the medical papyri that have survived from ancient Egypt consist of compilations of examinations, diagnoses and treatments. These documents have given scholars invaluable insights into Egyptian healing practices.

Hieroglyphic words used in medical terminology frequently contain clear visual references. Some signs depict a tumour or leaking tumour and indicate bodily discharges. The determinative sign in *mwt/moot*, the word for "death", is the image of a fallen man. Similarly, the verb "to spew out" *k3ʿ/kaha* contains an image of a man holding his hand to his mouth.

The Egyptians suffered from parasitic diseases such as schistosomiasis or bilharziasis, caused by a parasite in water

IN SICKNESS AND HEALTH

TO BE HEALTHY *snb/seneb* The verb "to be healthy" and the noun "health" are both written in the same way; they are determined by a scroll that may represent a medical document.

TO BE ILL *mr/mer* The determinative is a sparrow with tail pointed downward, a sign often used in words denoting negative concepts.

REMEDY *pẖrt/fert* The top-left symbol is a representation of the intestine, while the circular determinative may be the pupil of an eye.

PAIN *3hw/arhoo* A vulture, a reed shelter and a quail chick combine with a sparrow with downcast tail feathers.

TO SPEW OUT *kʿ/kaha* This is a variant of the word given in the main text (above). It shows a hillside, a forearm and liquid issuing from lips.

DOCTOR *swnw/soonoo* The word combines an arrow, a bowl, a stroke and a kneeling male figure. The arrow doubtless highlights the doctor's skill in treating injuries.

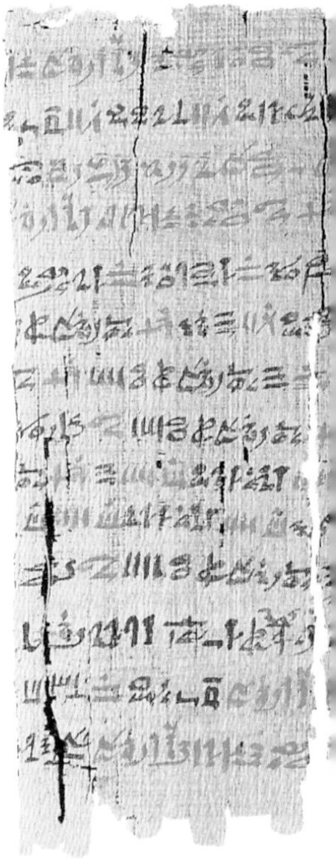

infiltrating the veins of the human host. They were also vulnerable to guinea worm and tapeworm. Bacterial and viral infections such as tuberculosis, tetanus, sepsis and abscesses, osteomyelitis, poliomyelitis and smallpox were common, as were snake and scorpion bites.

Doctors were required to undertake a formal training – according to some scholars they studied in a temple institution called a "house of life"; many held priestly titles, and were associated with Sekhmet, goddess of destruction and healing. Sometimes, doctors made use of healing spells. Magic was most frequently used in anti-venom spells: the patient was given water that had been poured over a stele inscribed with a magical text. But doctors were also skilled in bandaging and the use of poultices and potions.

Preventative medicine was also practised: garlic was used in spells for guarding a house, and would have provided some natural protection against mosquitoes. Purification rituals were used to prevent infestations of bugs and fleas.

Surviving ancient Egyptian medical papyri deal with broken bones, trauma wounds, childbirth and gynaecology. They contain both medical and magical remedies. The writing on this papyrus is in hieratic (see page 12).

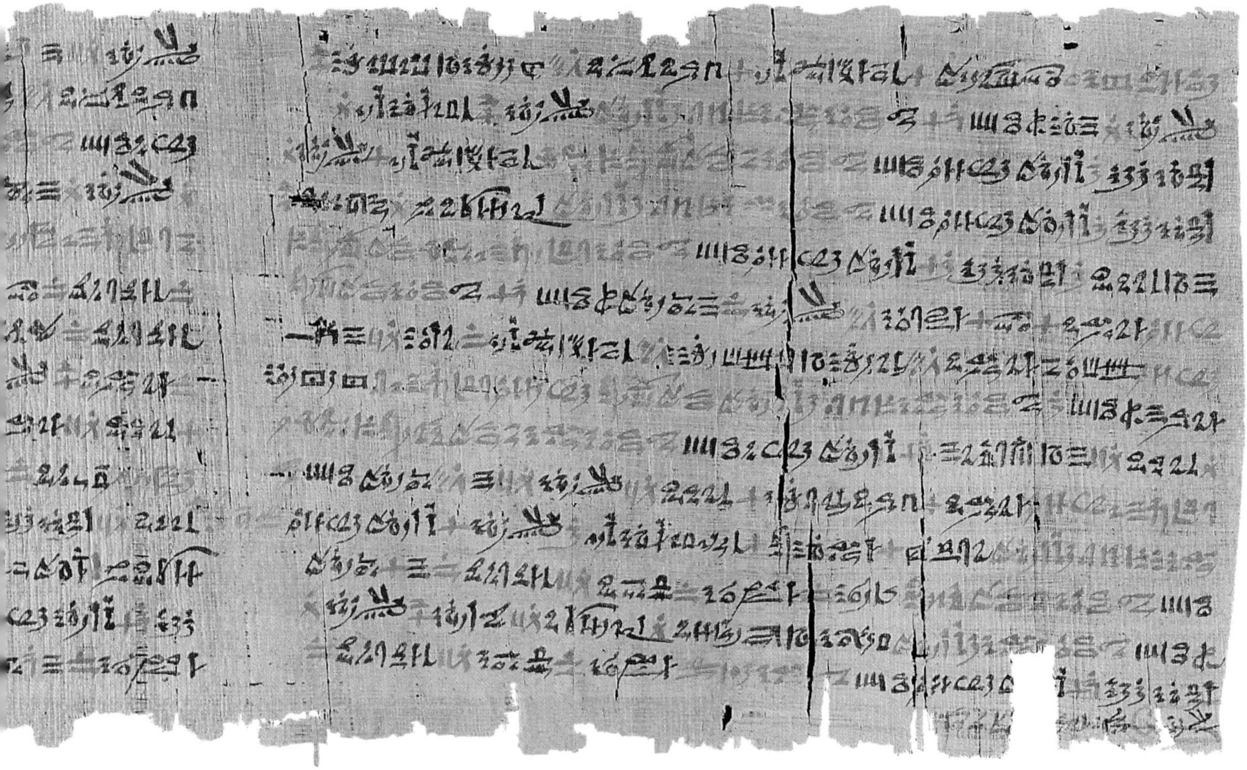

DEATH AND THE AFTERLIFE

A priest wearing the mask of Anubis, god of embalming, undertakes the funerary rituals of the deceased in this illustration from the Book of the Dead of Chensumose (10th–11th century BCE).

CENTRE *A detail of the shabtis pictured on page 101.*

A HIEROGLYPH FROM THE IMAGE OPPOSITE SHOWS A COBRA COILED ON A BASKET. THE REARING COBRA (CALLED THE URAEUS) WAS THE SYMBOL OF WADJET, GODDESS OF LOWER EGYPT, AND THIS HIEROGLYPHIC SIGN OF THE COBRA DETERMINED HER NAME; IT HAD NO PHONETIC VALUE. THE URAEUS WAS OFTEN SHOWN ON THE ROYAL CROWN REARING TO SPIT POISON AT THE KING'S ENEMIES.

Most ancient Egyptians believed that images of death held negative connotations, so they generally avoided hieroglyphic symbols of this nature – although signs relating to burial and bereavement do occasionally appear. Instead they tended to place emphasis on life, represented by the symbol ☥ *ꜥnk/annk*, and on the triumph of life over annihilation.

Surviving evidence of the funerary beliefs in early Egyptian times suggests that people believed life after death to be primarily reserved for the king and his family – the majority of the population had little to look forward to except a shadowy existence in the grave. The royals envisioned paradise as the abode of the great goddess of the winds, and in this "Field of Reeds" (also called the "Field of Offerings") they continued their earthly lives free of famine and disease. Only in the Middle Kingdom (1980–1630BCE) did people adopt a belief in eternal life for all as religious texts began to emphasize concepts of morality (see pages 72–73); Middle Kingdom funerary and instructional texts provided the correct responses for confronting the gods of the underworld. Some funerary deities were associated solely with the dead, while others played a wider role: Anubis was linked to embalming and mummification;Osiris, patron of the dead, was also associated with agricultural practices, while Hathor was linked to fertility, music and dance.

Preserving the corpse was essential to survival after death. The upper classes began their funeral preparations early, for life was uncertain and they had to commission, cut and decorate a tomb before they died. Images within these tombs show them at the peak of youth and fitness – these figures were a substitute for the physical body and were vital to survival. Hieroglyphic signs relating to funerary buildings and burial include the shrine : this symbol served as the determinative for the word *k3(r)i/kari* "chapel"; *mr/mer* represented a pyramid tomb, with the symbol of the pyramid as determinative, while the symbol of a double stairway was the determinative for the noun *k3y/kaee* "ascent".

Mummification, evident from the predynastic period onward, reached a peak of sophistication in the New Kingdom (1539–1075BCE) and began to decline after the Twenty-First Dynasty

(1075–945BCE). The embalming operation took seventy days. First the body was eviscerated: the heart remained in the body while the brain and inner organs were removed. Next the corpse was packed with natron salt and left for forty days, until it was totally desiccated. It was then washed, its cavities filled with resin, herbs and linen, then wrapped with linen strips. The stomach, liver, intestine and lungs were placed in canopic jars, often fashioned to resemble the four sons of Horus: Imseti, Hapi, Duamutef and Kebsenuef. Three signs of the mummified body were used to define the embalmed state and as a symbol of death.

A rearing cobra

They could also be used to refer to Osiris and the creator god Ptah. A casket sign was the determinative sign in the verb "to bury" *ḳrs/curse* and in the word for "coffin" *ḳrsw/cursu*.

The dead travelled to the underworld on a barge. On arrival they were examined by a tribunal in the presence of Osiris. The heart was thought to bear the weight of a person's conduct during life, and the deceased had to prove that their hearts were pure. In the Hall of Judgment their hearts were weighed against a feather – symbol of Maat, goddess of truth and justice. Thoth, the god of writing, recorded the outcome; those who failed this test might be consumed by a demon named "the devourer" (see page 72).

The deceased survived in more than one form. The *ba*, a spirit in the form of a human-headed bird, could travel to and from the tomb to interact with the living. The *ka* (soul) resided in the tomb and could be sustained with prayers and offerings; the upper classes employed priests to make sacrifices and present daily offerings at their relatives' tombs. If the heart was found to be pure when weighed against the feather of Maat in the Hall of Judgment before Osiris (see page 86), the *ba* and *ka* united to form the *akh*, which survived in that form throughout eternity and could be kind or vengeful toward the living.

The Egyptians recorded life events and family connections on monuments and stele. When tomb visitors read the inscribed text and spoke the deceased's name it contributed to the survival of the *ka*. Tomb images of the deceased were magical substitutes that could replace his or her physical body if it was damaged.

SURVIVAL IN THE UNDERWORLD

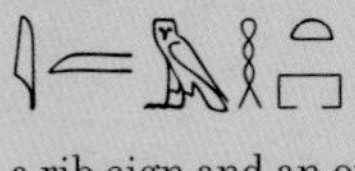

NETHERWORLD *imht/eemhet* A reed sign (*i*), a rib sign and an owl (*m*) combine with a twisted flax (*h*), a bread loaf (*t*) and a house sign in "netherworld".

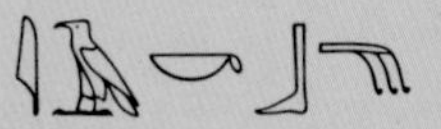

TO MOURN *i3kb/jarkeb* A flowering reed (*i*), a vulture (*3*), a basket with handle (*k*) and a leg and foot sign (*b*) spell the verb "to mourn". The hair is a determinative in words associated with emptiness or lack.

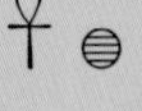

TO LIVE *ꜥnḫ/annk* The ankh sign for life combines with a water ripple (*n*) and a placenta (*ḫ*).

ETERNITY *nḥḥ/nekk* Two flax signs and a sun sign spell "eternity".

1 Ka

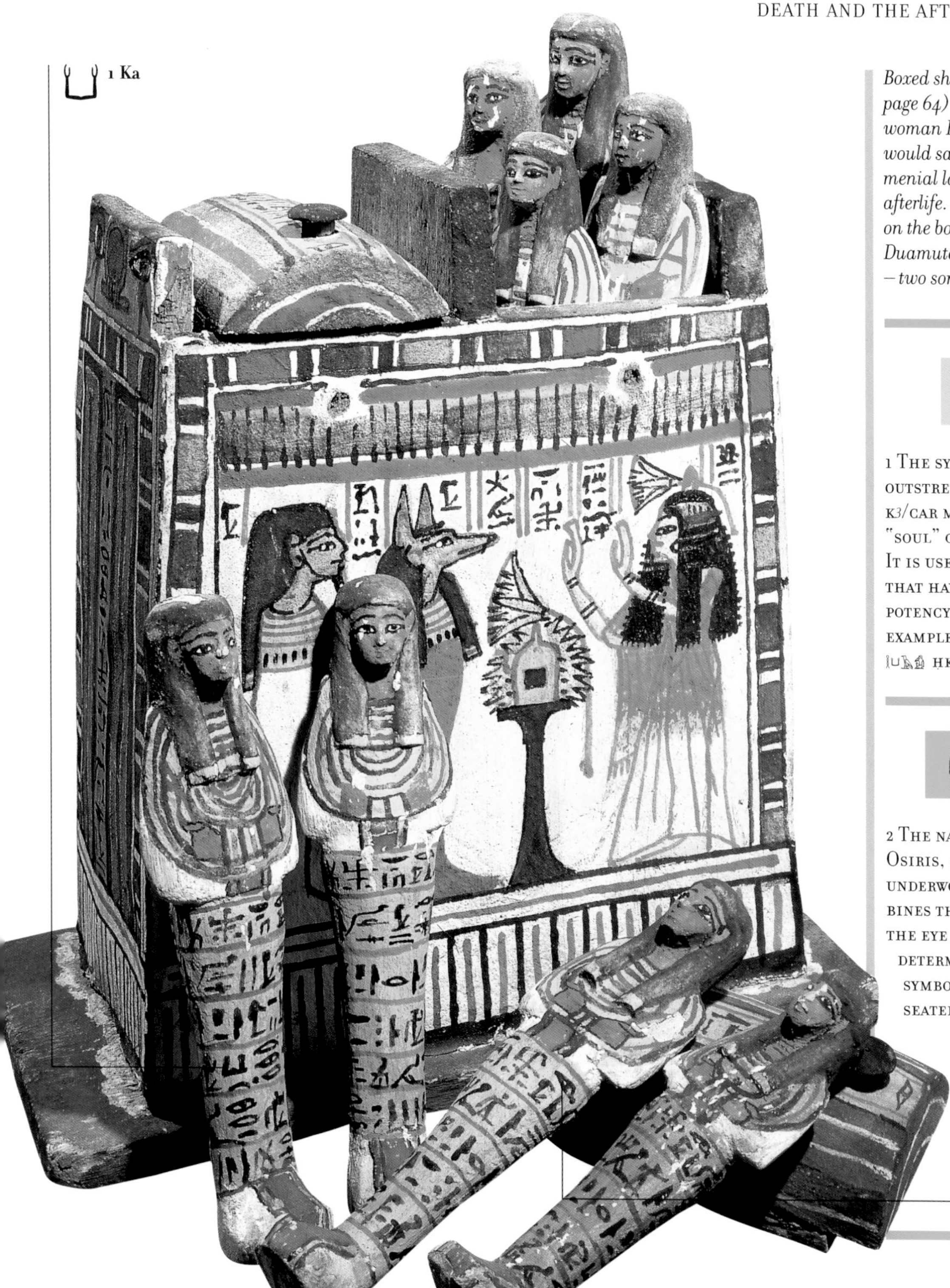

Boxed shabtis (see page 64) of the noblewoman Henutmehyt would save her from menial labour in the afterlife. She is shown on the box adoring Duamutef and Imseti – two sons of Horus.

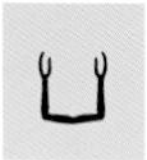

1 THE SYMBOL OF OUTSTRETCHED ARMS K3/CAR MEANS THE "SOUL" OR "SPIRIT". IT IS USED IN WORDS THAT HAVE MAGICAL POTENCY – FOR EXAMPLE, "MAGIC" HK3/HEKKA.

2 THE NAME OF OSIRIS, GOD OF THE UNDERWORLD, COMBINES THE THRONE, THE EYE AND THE DETERMINATIVE SYMBOL OF A SEATED GOD.

2 Osiris

RELATIONSHIPS

Wealthy family groups were often buried together, and tomb paintings frequently show the tomb owner surrounded by his wife and children, as in this image from a twelfth-century BCE tomb at Deir el-Medina showing the tomb builder Inherkha and family. The girl at the extreme left holds a bird resembling the hieroglyph for "duckling" – this was probably the child's family nickname.

PAGES 102–103: Ramesses II (c.1279–1213BCE) looks serenely out over the temple at Luxor. The ankh ☥ ꜥnh/annk *symbol of life and the conical loaf sign* di/dee *can be read on the base of the obelisk to the right of his statue.*

Egyptian art idealizes humans' relationships with the gods and with one another – portraits of married couples or family groups often emphasize the figures' closeness by depicting physical contact between them. Although emotive themes are otherwise rarely expressed through art, surviving literature and love poetry provide clues about the Egyptians' emotional and sexual mores.

GENERATIONS

The husband acted as the head of the Egyptian family. His wife was known by her first name followed by her married title, for example "Nefert, wife of Nakht".

Hieroglyphic words denoting family members always included the determinative figure of a man, woman or child. For example, a kneeling man is used to determine the word for "husband" *h3y/hay*, while "wife" *ḥmt/hemet* is determined by a seated female. Male and female determinatives also appear in "brother" *sn/sen* and "sister" *snt/senet*, words that were also used by friends and lovers as intimate terms of endearment (see also box, opposite).

The Egyptians favoured large families as the child mortality rate was high. Children were seen as vital for a family's future prosperity. The sign denoting a child, a youth shown with hand placed to mouth, determines the word for "child" *šrj/sherri* and one variant of "children" *msw/messo*.

There was no charitable care in ancient Egyptian communities, and individuals without families were often very needy – infertile women and childless widows were among the most vulnerable groups in the country. The elderly were looked after by their children or grandchildren. Life expectancy was not high: members of the lower classes, who tended to die earlier than their wealthy compatriots, were probably considered elderly at the age of forty years. The Egyptians rarely depicted old age in tomb images or other artistic representations. In hieroglyphic texts age was shown by the determinative of a man bent over a stick - .

FAMILY MEMBERS

FATHER *it/eat* A reed (*i*), a loaf (*t*), a snake (silent) and a man determinative spell "father".

MOTHER *mwt/moot* "Mother" uses a female determinative.

SON *s3/sar* A goose (*s3*) and a stroke (silent) spell *s3/sar*.

DAUGHTER *s3t/sat* A seated woman determines "daughter", spelled with goose (*s3*) and bread loaf (*t*).

EXPRESSING EMOTIONS

DETAIL, CENTRE: A painted limestone flake found at Deir el-Medina depicts mother love. A woman suckles her child while beneath a girl offers her cosmetics and a mirror. This ostraca (the term used for these flakes) dates from the Twentieth Dynasty (1196–1070BCE).

During most periods of Egyptian history, conventional art forms rarely portrayed feelings. These were considered better suited to the medium of poetry, which when written on papyrus would generally have been in hieratic rather than hieroglyphic script (see pages 12–13). However, all aspects of human emotions could be expressed through hieroglyphs.

Many words that dealt with emotive issues depicted gestures or jubilant actions. For example, the word denoting "love" *mri/merry* is accompanied by a man shown with his hand held to his mouth. The Egyptian term for "pleasure" or "affection" *st-ib/set-ib* uses the sign of the heart – already established as the universal symbol of love – as a determinative. The words for negative emotions, such as grief or anger, are often determined by figures performing appropriate gestures or body parts associated with demonstrating the emotions. The verb "to weep" *rmi/rem-ee* is determined by a weeping eye.

Some emotive words include images of animals that the ancient Egyptians associated with certain behavioural patterns: the monkey was used in the word for "fury" *knd/kend*; the crocodile in the adjective "aggressive"

THE LANGUAGE OF FEELINGS

TO CHARM *i3mt/yar-met* A tree, an owl, a bread loaf, a sealed document and three strokes spell out the verb "to charm".

TO BE HAPPY *mrr/mer* An owl, an arm and hand, a mouth, a tree and a sealed document are the signs used to write the verb "to be happy". The mouth had a clear visual connection with human expression of joy and happiness.

JUBILATION *ihhy/ee-hay* A reed, twin reed huts, twin reeds and a man with raised arms spell "jubilation". The male figure with raised arms was the generic determinative for words connected to celebration and to expressions of delight.

During the "Amarna period" (c.1390–1295BCE; see page 146) Egyptian artists produced innovative work portraying human emotions. Armana-period portraits of the royal family possess a rare naturalism, as evidenced by this unfinished statue of Akhenaten kissing a female figure thought to be one of his daughters.

3d/add; and the bull in the verb "to be angry" *ḏnd/jend.*

Mourning scenes depicted on tomb walls provide rare examples of emotional displays depicted in Egyptian art. Such images show groups of professional mourners throwing dirt on their clothes and tearing at their hair. Certain words associated with death and mourning used the hair symbol (see page 33). The hieroglyphic word for "mourning" *irtyw/erteoo* was composed of a reed, an eye, a vulture and a kneeling man with a hand to his lips. The vulture was linked to ill fate and death, although it did also have positive aspects (see page 36). The eye was a symbol of life; the Egyptians associated the closing of the eyes with death.

FORBIDDEN LOVE

Relationships that did not have family approval were firmly discouraged. Thwarted love was the theme of this New Kingdom (1539–1075BCE) poem:

"The voice of the
wild goose shrills,
It is caught by its bait;
My love of you pervades me,
I cannot loosen it.
I shall retrieve my nets,
But what do I tell
my mother,
To whom I go daily,
Laden with bird catch?
I have spread no snares today,
I am caught in my love of you!"

LOVE AND FAMILY LIFE

The dying Osiris provides the sperm that will make Isis pregnant with Horus, the prototype of Egypt's divine kings (see page 82). This basalt relief is from the fourth century BCE *sarcophagus of the royal scribe Nes-Shutfere at Saqqara.*

Sexual themes and erotic elements featured widely in Egyptian myth, in papyri, in statuary and in art. In the "Amarna period" when King Amenhotep IV (1353–1336BCE) attempted a cultural and religious revolution (see page 146), artists emphasized the body's curves and expressed relationships through sensual expositions. Their idealized representations show men and women in their finest attire, the contours of the upper body and hips accentuated.

The hair *šny/sheny* was associated with both male and female sexuality, while an eye with eyeliner was used as determinative in the word "beautiful" *ꜥn/een*. The face could also highlight the pleasure the Egyptians derived from appearance, as shown by the similarity between the words for "face" *ḥnt/henet* and "to take pleasure" *ḥntš/hentesh*.

Records suggest that the ancient Egyptians took a tolerant attitude to sexual matters, accepting prostitution, adultery and homosexual acts in certain circumstances – although as a general rule married individuals were expected to remain chaste and relationships between same-sex couples were frowned on. A liberal approach seldom extended to portraying sexual intercourse in formal art. Temple scenes of divine conception often show the god and queen seated on a bed or a plinth as he embraces her or lifts the *ꜥnḫ/annk* (sign of life) to her nose. In

MATTERS OF THE HEART

TO KISS *sn/sen* The word combines a barbed arrowhead, a water ripple and a profile of a human face. The face is a generic determinative for words associated with joy.

TO BEGET *wtt/oo-t* A quail chick (*w*) and two bread loaves (*tt*) combine to spell *wtt*. The phallus is the determinative sign.

TO BECOME PREGNANT *iwr/ewer* A kid or goat (*i*), a sparrow (*wr*) and a mouth (*r*) spell *iwr*. The word is determined by the symbol of a woman in a posture associated by the Egyptians with giving birth.

TO EMBRACE *inḳ/ink* Reed, fish, water and hill spell *inḳ*. Embracing arms determine the word.

illustrations of the resurrection of Osiris, a bird hovering above Osiris's phallus refers to his impregnation of Isis with the child that will become the falcon god Horus, conqueror of the child's wicked uncle Seth. Generally in temple scenes, fertility and birth are suggested by symbols representing the sexual organs of animals or humans: 𓂑 *mnḏ/menj* the "breast", 𓂐 *ḥmt/hemet* the female sexual organ and 𓂸 or 𓂺 *ḥnn/hen* "phallus".

A few examples of erotic art have survived: Queen Hatshepsut (*c.*1479–1458BCE) is featured in sexually explicit graffiti in the cliffs above her temple at Deir el Bahri, while on the walls of New Kingdom (1539–1075BCE) temples, the god Min may be seen holding his phallus.

TRADES AND SKILLS

Male members of the Egyptian upper classes, many of whom were literate, often acted as scribes, priests or state officials. Many men from the lower social classes were farmers, but others learned a trade and became craftsmen, miners or soldiers. Men and women worked as servants.

This scene from the Eighteenth Dynasty (c.1539–1292BCE) Theban tomb of the sculptors Nebamun and Ipuki depicts craftsmen in a royal workshop. The central figure in the lower section holds a scribe's palette with red and black inks; the hieroglyphic symbol for the palette is written in the right column above his head. The figures in the upper section make wooden carvings of the djed column.

MINING

The ancient Egyptians were experts in the excavation and mining of stone, minerals and metals. Various types of stone were needed for monuments, statuary and funerary objects, while minerals, semi-precious stones and precious metals were required to adorn buildings, statues, ornaments and jewelry.

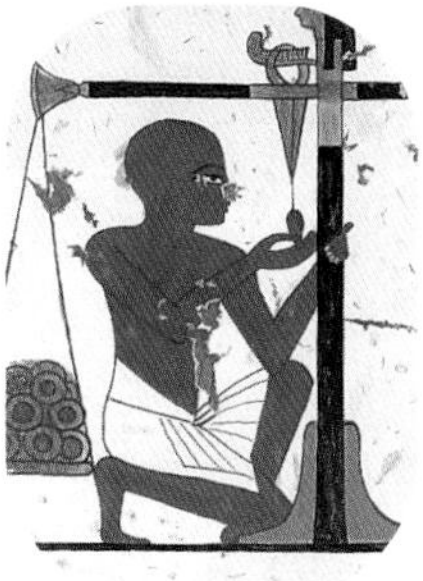

DETAIL, CENTRE: *Another part of the above tomb painting shows a craftsman weighing gold, probably from a mine in the Eastern Desert or in Nubia.*

To supply these materials, mining expeditions involving as many as 10,000 miners, craftsmen, masons and labourers were regularly dispatched to regions beyond the Nile Valley, such as the Eastern Desert and Nubia (to mine gold) and the Sinai (in search of turquoise).

The hieroglyphic sign denoting "miner" *ik/ek* was composed of a flowering reed, a basket with handle, and a man leaning on a stick, usually the generic determinative for words associated with old age. In the word for "quarry" or "mine" *ḫ3t/hart* a block of stone was used as a determinative; the other signs are a fish and a bread loaf. Mining tools could also be used to determine related words – the chisel determined the verb "to carve" *mnḫ/menek*.

Among the most common signs used to denote the precious metals for which the miners were digging were a series of pellets that represented balls of metal or stone. They appear in the words for "gold" *nbw/neboo*, "turquoise" *mfk3t/mef-kar-t* and a single pellet is in *msdmt/mes-demet*, the mineral that the Egyptians used in the production of the black eye paint, kohl.

SERVANTS OF THE GODS

Some priests worked full-time in the temple, but others were part-time and served there for one month in four, devoting the other three months to a secular occupation. The word for "a priest serving his time in the temple" *wnwt/wenoot* includes the religious symbol of the star placed above a sun sign to indicate the passage of time.

In the temple, priests often performed ritual sacrifices. The hieroglyph for "libation priest" *ibḥ/eebah* includes the sign of a goat or kid, an animal frequently sacrificed in the temple. The priests also dealt with temple administration and were responsible for training candidates to the priesthood.

Cleanliness was of the highest importance for a priest. Most temples had a sacred lake, where the priest was expected to undergo ritual purification before officiating. He was shaved of all body hair, and after bathing put on the finest linen garments and fresh sandals; he avoided wool and leather, which were considered impure.

PRIESTS AND TEMPLE LIFE

PRIEST *wꜥb/wab* The hieroglyphic word for "priest" includes the symbol of the water pot and a series of water currents, indicating the ritual practice of cleanliness associated with the priesthood.

PRIESTHOOD *wnwt/wenoot* The plural sign of short vertical strokes indicates a collection of priests. The word includes a hare, a ripple of water and a pot. The determinative sign is a star, a familiar symbol among words of a religious nature.

OR

PRAISE *i3w/jaw* The determinative in both variants of this word is a man in an attitude of adoration.

TEMPLE CHANTRESS *šmꜥit/shemeet* The sedge plant sign, associated with the south, can also represent Egyptian music. It is accompanied by reeds and the loaf sign.

To ensure that his words would be pure when addressing the gods, he rinsed out his mouth with water and natron – the type of salt used in mummification.

The priests also had many roles outside the temple. They worked in funerary cults and attended the embalming of the dead, dedicated statues, buildings and objects, and presided at festivals, where they carried statues of the gods and goddesses on portable shrines in procession. There is even some evidence to suggest that priests could wage war on behalf of the gods, for they were often affiliated with the army's élite archer corps. In addition to their religious positions, priests were professional members of society, employed in the public sector as doctors, architects or court

This sphinx of Amenemhet III (c.1818–1772BCE) sat in the temple of Bastet, the cat goddess. It was reinscribed by Ramesses II (c.1279–1213BCE).

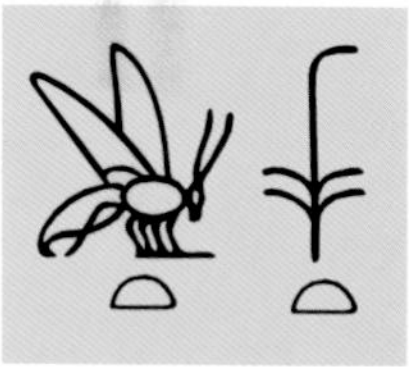

1 BEE AND 2 SEDGE PLANT (TOGETHER "NESOO BEET") SPELL "THE KING OF UPPER AND LOWER EGYPT". THE PHRASE WAS THE TRADITIONAL EPITHET OF EGYPTIAN KINGS.

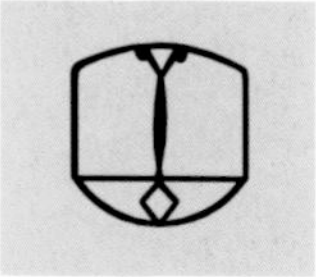

3 THIS SIGN, WHICH RESEMBLES A SQUARE ABOVE AN OVAL BOWL (ḤB/HEB) IS THE WORD FOR A RELIGIOUS FESTIVAL OR FEAST.

As intermediary between Egypt and the gods, the king was the land's chief priest (see page 60). This carving depicts Nectanebo I (381–362BCE) presenting a statue of the goddess Maat to Thoth in baboon form.

officials. Some priests acquired great reputations. Khaemwaset, fourth son of Ramesses II (*c.*1279–1213BCE), was a celebrated early archeologist, who restored Old Kingdom (2625–2130BCE) monuments that were ancient even in his day. The priests offered no moral guidance: their role was to maintain universal order and win divine approval through ritual.

Priestly status was often hereditary. By the Nineteenth Dynasty (1292–1190BCE), even the powerful position of High Priest of Amun – who officiated for the king – was passed from father to son. Relations between priesthood and sovereign could be problematic and religious and political factions were involved in power struggles. At the end of the Twentieth Dynasty (*c.*1075BCE), the priests of Amun Re ruled Upper Egypt.

The title of priestess may have been honorary, for royal women were often called "priestesses of Hathor". However, in early periods of Egyptian history women of the higher social classes do appear to have taken part in temple ritual. They were described as *hemet netjer* or *wabet*, the female equivalent of the title for priest *wꜥb/wab*.

During the New Kingdom (1539–1075BCE), women did not hold priestly titles but were linked to the temple by the name *shemayet* ("musician"). In tomb paintings the women are shown with a *sistrum* – a rattle sacred to the goddess Hathor. The holder of the prestigious title "god's wife of Amun" was expected to pacify the god by shaking her *sistrum* and arousing his desire. In the Eighteenth Dynasty (1539–1292BCE), the daughter of the High Priest of Amun was often known as *duat netjet* ("divine adoratrice"), but the title may have been an honorary one.

SERVANTS OF THE STATE

The most important official in ancient Egypt was the vizier, who controlled the administration of the country, was in charge of building programmes and acted as chief architect. Although only one vizier was usually appointed, two posts were sometimes created for the separate governing of Upper and Lower Egypt. The vizier was traditionally regarded as a man of wisdom; instruction texts often purport to recount the moral teachings of the vizier to his son. The word for "vizier" *ṯ3ty/charty* includes the depiction of a duckling (*ṯ3*) and a bread loaf (*t*) and a single stroke; it is determined by the seated figure of a man, indicating that it was a position held by men.

Local mayors or governors, who were appointed to rule towns or villages throughout Egypt, were answerable to the vizier. The word for "mayor" *ḥ3ty-ʿ/harty-ah* includes the head and front of a lion above an outstretched arm and hand, indicating a man who is placed at the forefront of power.

In addition an extensive bureaucracy ran the treasuries, granaries and law courts. A network of "kenbet councils" throughout the country was reponsible for property, its ownership and its transference; they interpreted disputes and arranged settlements within communities. The councils were run by the mayors or local chiefs, who had the power to

OFFICIALS

OFFICIAL *sr/seer* The word combines a folded cloth (*s*) and a mouth (*r*) and is determined by a man with a stave. The stave was an object traditionally associated with elders or men of wisdom in Egypt.

COURTIER *smr/ smear* The word for "courtier" includes a chisel, an owl, a mouth and a seated figure.

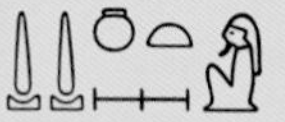
MAGISTRATE *ḏ3ḏ3t/jarjart* The word may indicate the sound of chattering voices. It includes two signs that represent fire drills, an irrigation channel, a pot and a bread sign. It can also be translated "assessor".

LORD *nb/neb* A wickerwork basket sign stands for the sound *nb*; placed above the head of a seated man, it indicates a person who owns land.

In the Fifth Dynasty (2500–2350BCE), an official named Ty achieved great wealth and status. In life he was in charge of two pyramids and a number of solar temples, and in death he was honoured in a fine mastaba tomb at North Saqqara. This statue stood in the serdab, a chamber in the tomb, where the priests of Ty's mortuary cult made food and incense offering to the deceased's ka.

prosecute criminals. Viziers and their representatives frequently visited towns in order to check and register the activities of these local officials.

Members of the king's family were appointed to the highest ranks of the official hierarchy and secured influential careers within the military or as priests. The vizier himself was often related to the royal family. During the New Kingdom (1539–1075BCE), governors were sent abroad to control areas of political importance beyond the borders of Egypt. The governors secured the subservience of vassal states through annual tribute or taxation. If the foreign "subjects" refused to comply, the army was sent to quell what the Egyptians described as a "rebellion" of the enemy state.

Men and women of the upper social classes were rewarded for their service with royal gifts and titles. The word for a "noble" *špsi/shepsoo* includes a seated man who carries a baton of authority and a folded cloth that is a symbol of prosperity; the word is determined by a roll of papyrus. Military men were presented with prizes of armour, slaves and gold. In tomb and temple depictions of these award ceremonies, the king and members of the royal family were shown throwing the smaller gifts from a palace balcony. In the courtyard below, the fanbearers and officers of the household led the recipients to their places beneath the king.

A LIFE OF WORK

Most Egyptians in the lower social classes were farmers; others worked as stonemasons, miners and builders. Hieroglyphic symbols often denoted a person's occupation, using human figures shown in recognizable places or activities. For example, the word for "peasant" *sḫty/sharty* shows a field of reeds, a loaf, two strokes and a man crouched on the ground, indicating a clear association between farmer and field.

Wooden models found in tombs of the Middle Kingdom (2040–1640BCE) depict workers spinning, dyeing, baking, brewing and preparing meat. Scenes in the tomb of Rekhmire, governor of Thebes in the reign of King Tuthmosis III (1479–1425BCE), show goldsmiths, leatherworkers, jewellers and sculptors at work.

Many workers were employed as servants in the houses of the wealthy. Women were employed to cook, make bread and clean the house. Men and women worked as wigmakers and coiffeurs and women as beauticians, waiting upon upper-class women. Wealthy women hired wetnurses: the word for "wetnurse" *mnꜥt/men-art*

SERVANTS, SLAVES AND WORKERS

POOR MAN *nḏs/nedjes* The word incorporates the sign of a water ripple (*n*), a cobra shown in repose(*ḏ*) and a folded cloth (*s*), together with a bird of unfavourable omen and a crouching man who belongs to the lower classes.

SERVANT *ḥry-pr/hary pear* The word *ḥr* often indicates "one who is in" while *pr* is translated "house".

MAID *idit/eedeet* The word includes the signs of the reed, the hand and the bread sign (*t*), together with the symbol of a child holding a finger to his or her mouth.

MANSERVANT *b3k/back* The jabiru (the bird (*b3*) associated the *ba* – see page 98) is used in conjunction with a reed basket with a handle (*k*). The determinative is a man of low rank.

BAKER *rtḥty/ret-harty* The forked stave is believed to be an object used in breadmaking; it combines with a bread loaf sign, two strokes and a man striking with a stick.

COMMONERS *rḫyt/recheet* The word *rḫ* which means "to know", combines with the image of a lapwing – one of the commonest birds in ancient Egypt.

In a fifteenth-century BCE *wall painting of a banquet scene from the tomb in western Thebes of the astronomer priest and scribe Nakht, a servant girl offers perfume to guests.*

includes the sign of a female breast; the determinative is a nurse breastfeeding.

The sign for washerman *rẖty/ rakhty* includes the image of a man of low rank. The washing of clothes was invariably undertaken by males. The hieroglyphic word for manservant or "butler" *wdpw/wedpoo* includes a beer jar, a quail chick and a man in a crouching position.

Servants and slaves belonged to distinct classes. Slaves were taken from many areas of life: the lower classes were sometimes forced to sell family members into slavery, while criminals and foreigners were conscripted as slaves. Foreign slaves captured during military campaigns were presented to the king in fetters, then often given to soldiers as rewards for valour. An owner had the right to hire out or sell his slaves. While slaves were assigned to owners, servants chose to work for certain employers. Slaves, however, could marry and were permitted to conduct business with the same rights as free members of society.

SOLDIERS

In the New Kingdom (1539–1075BCE) – the only period for which details of ancient Egyptian military organization survive – the army was composed of companies of 200 footsoldiers (consisting of twenty ten-man platoons). Companies were grouped into divisions of around 5,000 men under the banner of their local god. Charioteers were élite members of the army divisions. Officers were recruited from among literate, well-educated young men from the upper social classes, and trained for leadership. Egyptian words for military leaders are often distinguished by the symbols associated with their rank. The hieroglyph for "unit commander" *ṯsw/chesoo* uses the sign for the girdle or knot *ṯst/chest* that a commander wore as an emblem of his office.

Many troops were professional soldiers – although there is evidence to suggest that conscripts served alongside them. The most feared military units were the archers, armed with the powerful composite longbow (see pages 80-81). The sign for "bowman" *mšʿ/mesha* shows a figure kneeling in the position often adopted by archers in battle. This sign is also used to determine *mnfyt/menfet* "soldiers".

As well as archery, military instructors taught swordsmanship, hand-to-hand combat and drill. Troops were issued with

WORDS OF WAR

TO FIGHT *ʿḥ3/a-har-ah* A pair of arms holding a shield and a mace, a vulture and a man with a stave make up the verb "to fight".

TO DESTROY *ḥḏi/hed-ji* A stave with a pear-shaped mace head combines with a cobra and crossed sticks to spell *ḥḏi*. The word is determined by a sparrow shown with tailfeathers pointing down.

ENEMY *ḫfty/hefty* A placenta, a horned snake, a bread loaf and plural strokes form the word for "enemy". It is determined by a conquered figure falling to the ground.

SOLDIER *wʿw/oo-ah-oo* A quail chick with an arm, another quail chick and a hand clasping a stick spell *wʿw*. The arm symbol also appears in the word for "strong".

weapons from the state armories. During long marches, large caches of weapons and supplies were transported on wheeled vehicles.

The crops and food resources pillaged from conquered territories provided an important source of additional sustenance for soldiers. For this reason the Egyptians preferred to wage campaigns during the harvest months, when large land armies could be sustained in this way. Ration cards were issued in the form of wooden tallies, and the state also provided troops with warm blankets and lengths of linen fabric that were wound around the body and used as armour. However, according to one New Kingdom text, supplies were insufficient: "Come let me tell you the woes of being a soldier ... He is hungry, his belly hurts ... He may not rest. There are no clothes, no sandals ... He drinks water every third day."

A limestone relief from the reign of Amenhotep IV (c.1353–1336BCE) depicts soldiers on the move. The lefthand soldier carries spear, axe and shield, the typical arms of New Kingdom infantry; his comrade holds a lasso.

WEAPONS AND WAR

This model of a troop of forty soldiers carrying shields and spears was made for the tomb of the Middle Kingdom (c.1980–1630BCE) nomarch (local ruler) Meseheti at Asyut. Tombs of the Middle Kingdom era are rich in military texts and images of soldiers.

Egypt's generally inhospitable landscape and desert borders provided a natural defence against invasion. But the ancient Egyptians had a distrust of foreigners that gave them a strong incentive from the predynastic period onward to develop an intimidating military. By the Eighteenth Dynasty (1539–1292BCE), the Egyptian army was a supreme force that dominated the region.

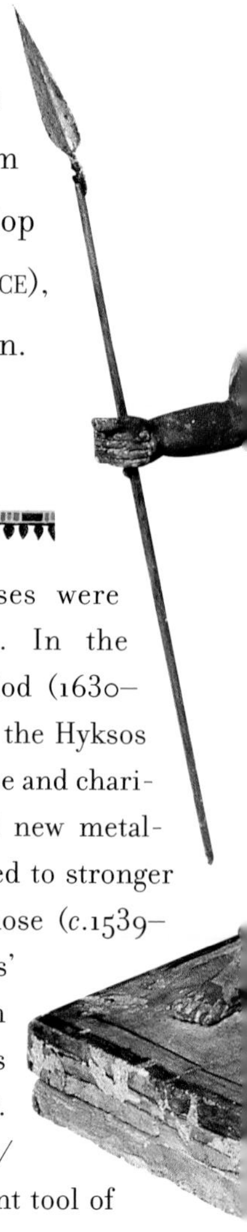

THE FORCE OF EGYPT

In the Old Kingdom (2625–2130BCE), an organized force of fighting men was supported by formations of archers. Early campaigns were mobilized by Sneferu – (*c*.2625–2585BCE) in one expedition to Nubia, he captured 7,000 prisoners and more than 200,000 head of cattle.

In the First Intermediate Period (2130–1980BCE), local rulers vied for control over central government: it was a violent period, when war became a way of life. Mentuhotep II (*c*.2081–2075BCE) – the founder of the Eleventh Dynasty – declared himself the king of a unified Egypt. He led expeditions against the Libyans and campaigned into Sinai, while his son built fortresses along the Delta borders to protect Egypt against the Asiatics. During the Middle Kingdom (1980–1630BCE), fortresses were built throughout Nubia. In the Second Intermediate Period (1630–1539BCE), invaders named the Hyksos popularized the use of horse and chariot in war and introduced new metal-working techniques that led to stronger swords and daggers. Ahmose (*c*.1539–1514BCE) used the invaders' weapons against them when he drove the Hyksos out of Egypt in *c*.1535BCE. The chariot *wrrt/warret* became an important tool of the Egyptian army. Many of Ahmose's successors had military careers, including Tuthmosis III (*c*.1479–1425BCE), who left an extensive account of the battle plans of his reign (see page 124).

MILITARY RECORDS

Ramesses II (c.1279–1213BCE) prepares to execute prisoners on this stele. Two details taken from the area behind the pharaoh's back are reproduced below.

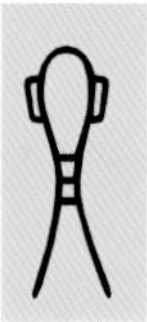

THE SIGN OF A LOOP OF CORD WAS ASSOCIATED WITH PROTECTION. RAMESSES II'S MILITARY MIGHT PROTECTED EGYPT AGAINST FOREIGNERS.

THIS IMAGE OF THREE PAPYRUS REEDS WAS ASSOCIATED WITH THE DELTA. IN MIDDLE EGYPTIAN IT WAS OFTEN REPLACED WITH , AS IN *T3-MḤW/TAA-MAHOO*, "THE DELTA".

A large body of ancient Egyptian documents, letters and military literature survives, providing details of Egypt's military campaigns and foreign relations. In the New Kingdom (1539–1075BCE), rulers used temple inscriptions and images to make a public exhibition of Egypt's military might. The Annals of Tuthmosis III (*c*.1479–1425BCE), a series of texts inscribed on the walls of the Temple of Amun-Re at Karnak, are the record of seventeen campaigns and cover tactical aspects of Egyptian military engagement. One inscription describes Tuthmosis at the head of his army as "like Horus, the smiter, lord of power" and declares that "Amun strengthened his arms" as he triumphed over the Asiatics at Meggido.

Temple inscriptions also survive of Ramesses II's campaign against the Hittites in the summer of 1274BCE. Ramesses rallied his troops at Pi-Ramesse, his official residence in *t3-mḥw/taa-mahoo*, the Delta, then led his army overland through Canaan and southern *rṯnw/retenoo*, Syria. His support troops were sent along the Phoenecian coast, where they intended to cut across land and rendezvous with the king at Kadesh in Syria. The army was divided into four divisions, one named after each of the four gods Amun , Re , Ptah and Seth . While still a few miles from Kadesh, Ramesses took the First Division of Amun, and set off in front of his army. He was joined by Shosu tribesmen who professed loyalty to the Egyptian cause.

The men informed him that the enemy, the Hittites, were hiding in the land of Aleppo 120 miles (190km) to the north. Ramesses, greatly pleased by this news, set up camp on a site near the town he planned to besiege. However, as he was putting up his tents, scouts checking the area came upon two Hittite spies who confessed to having given false information about the whereabouts of the Hittite army. The men of the Hittite kingdom *ḫt/hati* were in fact mobilizing less than 2 miles (3km) away.

The Division of Re was now arriving, but the other units of Ramesses's army were still several miles away. Just as the Egyptian king was discussing an emergency plan with his army leaders, the Hittite chariots appeared and ploughed into the unprepared ranks of the Division of Re. The king's unit panicked, but according to the royal records Ramesses "shone like Montu" (the god of war) as he put on his coat of armour and leaped into his chariot. He charged alone into the opposing ranks, driving back the enemy.

EGYPT AND BEYOND

The Nile is the world's longest continuously flowing river. It flows through Egypt for only the final third of its 4,000-mile (6,500 km) length from the East African highlands to the Mediterranean Sea. The relief carving represents the union of Upper and Lower Egypt and was made on the base of one of the statues of Ramesses II (c.1279–1213BCE) at Abu Simbel. The two figures are of Hapy, god of the Nile flood; the top cartouche contains Ramesses's prenomen and the lower one, his nomen (see page 85). The righthand side of the lower cartouche spells "beloved of Re", which reads as "Ramesses"; the lefthand side reads "beloved of Amun".

Egypt is "the gift of the Nile", wrote the Greek historian Herodotus in the fifth century BCE. Without the river, Egypt would be desert. Silt deposited by the Nile's annual flood made farming possible, but the extent of flooding was uncertain – and while low floods could lead to famine, high floods caused damage in fields and villages. The unpredictable Nile dominated the ancient Egyptians' view of their country and of the world – and probably caused the desire for order to loom so large in their myths and religion.

THE BLACK LAND

The black silt deposited by the river gave Egypt its ancient name – *kmt/kemet*, "the black land". The Nile that brings life to the Egyptian soil is in fact a derivative of two rivers – the Blue Nile, which rises in Lake Tana, Ethiopia, and is filled with silt during the summer rains, and the White Nile, which derives its main flow from Lake Victoria and joins the Blue Nile at Khartoum, the capital of the modern Republic of Sudan.

Within Egypt, the river is composed of two sections (see map opposite) – the long, sinuous Valley and the Delta (so named by the Greeks because the shape reminded them of the fourth letter of their alphabet Δ, inverted). In the Delta region, the river branches into a network of channels until it meets the sea. One branch runs to the Faiyum region – used by the ancient Egyptian kings as hunting ground and burial site. The Egyptians regarded the desert that bordered the Nile Valley with foreboding. Because of its scorched aridity, they called the desert the "red land" *dšrt/deshret*.

The Nile provided the Egyptians with their most efficient means of transport. Vessels travelling north relied on the current while those heading south hoisted sails to take advantage of the prevailing wind, which blows from the north. As a result the word *ẖdi/heddi* "to go north" was determined by a boat without sails, while *ḫnti/hek-en-ty* "to go south" depicted a boat with sails.

"Strong in truth is Re, Chosen of Re"

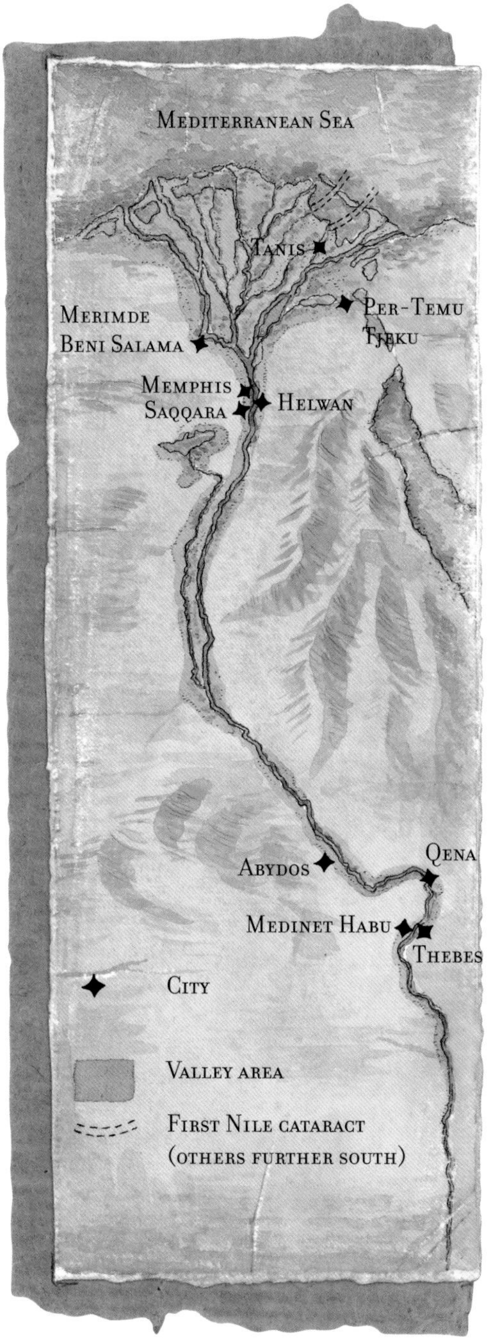

"Ramesses, Beloved of Amun"
(although the scribe has used two folded cloths to complete the phrase, it should correctly appear as here and on page 85)

THE FORTY-TWO NOMES

King Menkaure (c.2532–2510BCE) stands between the goddess Hathor (left) and a figure representing the seventeenth nome of Upper Egypt. The text at the king's foot reads "Ruler of Upper and Lower Egypt, Menkaure, eternally beloved"; the words at Hathor's feet are in praise of the goddess.

Ancient Egypt was divided into forty-two nomes or provinces. Nomes evolved from village communities that were controlled by independent rulers called mayors or nomarchs. Gradually, the villages amalgamated into large districts that developed cultural and religious identities. The word for "nome" *sp3t/spat* combined the signs of the folded cloth, a stool, a bread loaf, and land marked by irrigation channels.

Totem emblems, which often included agricultural symbols, were mounted on banners like district flags, while parochial symbols were recorded on objects of art. Pots from the early predynastic period (fourth millennium BCE) bear emblems of boats and images of gods and shrines, many relating to Hathor in her role as a cattle goddess. During periods of economic growth and cultural exchange between regions the deities of particular nomes became more widely popular. With the amalgamation of the provinces, myths and divine statuary or other images were exchanged by members of different regional groups.

In the Old Kingdom (2625–2130BCE), the Egyptians began to record the names of their governors. During the Fifth and Sixth Dynasties (2500–2350BCE and 2350–2170BCE), each administrative area was controlled by one man, who was known as the "chief of the nome".

These local chiefs – who sometimes also held priestly titles – assimilated a great deal of wealth and power and became indispensable members of the Egyptian administrative system. As time progressed, the nomarchs gained the type of power that had once been the preserve of the king alone and their power brought them into conflict with one another. Their feuding eventually drew Egypt into civil war during the years of the First Intermediate Period (2130–1980BCE). The titles and symbols associated with the unification of Upper and Lower Egypt were remarkably enduring. For example, the royal title *nsw-bit/nsw-bity* "King of Upper and Lower Egypt" was in use from the unification of the country in *c.*3000BCE for more than 2,000 years beyond the Nineteenth Dynasty (1292–1190BCE). The sign combines the sedge plant, emblem of Upper Egypt, and the bee, emblem of Lower Egypt.

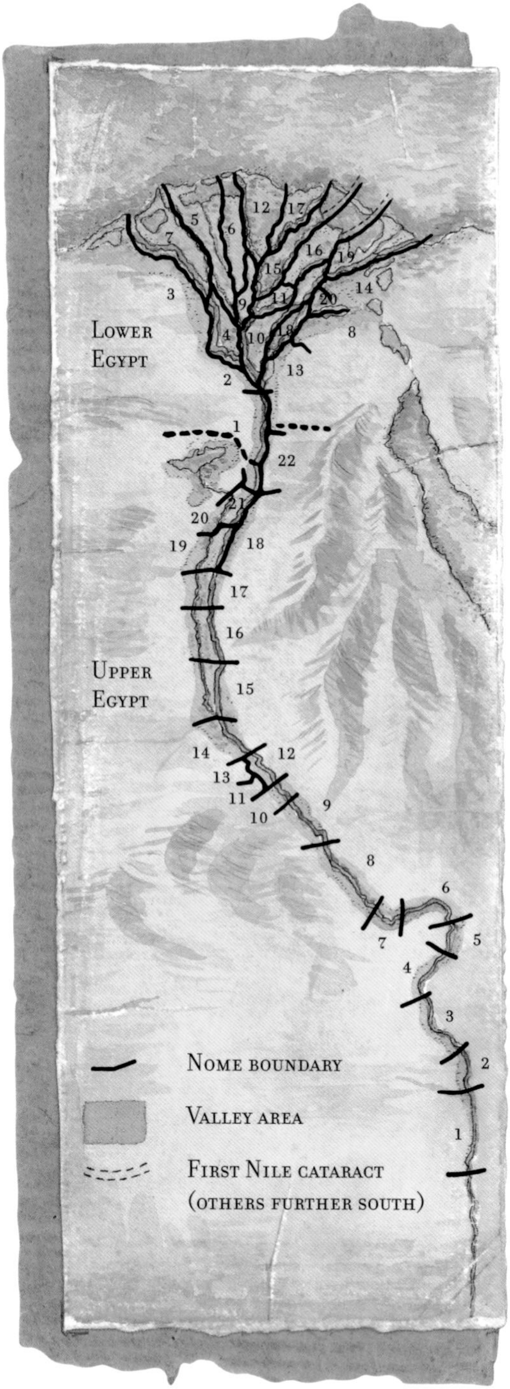

THE NOMES: SELECTED ENSIGNS

An ensign or symbol was associated with each of the 42 nomes, and in statuary representatives of the nomes were depicted wearing the relevant ensigns on their heads – see, for example, the statue wearing the ensign of the 17th nome of Upper Egypt opposite. The following are a selection of the ensigns that were in use during the Greco-Roman period (332BCE–CE395). The numbers refer to those on the map of the nomes (left).

UPPER EGYPT

Nome 1 Flat land with grains of sand above an unclassified sign

Nome 4 A sceptre decorated with a fillet and a feather

Nome 5 The falcon, symbol of the god Horus, repeated

Nome 7 The sistrum, a rattle sacred to the goddess Hathor used by priestesses in the temple

Nome 8 A wig attached to a pole

Nome 12 The image of a mountain plus the horned viper sign.

Nome 13 A sycamore tree, a viper and the image of three waterpots in a rack

Nome 15 A desert hare

Nome 19 The image of a leg and foot flanked by two sceptres bearing the image of an animal

Nome 22 A knife sharpener

LOWER EGYPT

Nome 1 A wall plus a mace with a pear-shaped head

Nome 2 The foreleg of an ox

Nome 3 A falcon and a feather on a type of standard which was used for carrying religious symbols

Nome 15 The sacred ibis

Nome 17 An elephant's tusk, a hand, a bread loaf and a town determinative

SACRED SITES

Protected by his sister-wife Isis, Osiris grasps the royal crook and flail and wears the plumed atef crown (in which he is commonly depicted) in a detail from the Book of the Dead of the scribe Ani of c.1290BCE. Before him the four sons of Horus stand atop a lotus flower. As god of resurrection and death, Osiris was worshipped at the burial grounds of Abydos.

DETAIL, CENTRE: *Isis holds the ankh or sign of life.*

Along the banks of the Nile, the ancient Egyptian landscape was dotted with monumental temples dedicated to the cults of prominent local and national gods. Within the temple walls, members of an élite priesthood appeased the gods and gave them sustenance, so ensuring Egypt's continuing well-being. Thriving towns and cities tended to grow up around these important sacred sites, often lending them political as well as religious significance.

The capital of the thirteenth Lower Egyptian nome (see page 128), Heliopolis (now a northern suburb of Cairo) was one of ancient Egypt's most important and influential religious sites. It was primarily associated with the sun god Re, Re-Atum or Re-Horakhty – the name Heliopolis comes from ancient Greek *helios*, "sun". Its ancient Egyptian name was "Iunu", written *ᶜIwnw/oo-noo* in hieroglyphs. The site saw the emergence of the "Heliopolitan doctrine", which cast Atum and Re as the primary creator deities (see page 145).

To the south of Heliopolis lay Memphis, the capital of Egypt for most of the country's ancient history. The name Memphis comes from the ancient Greek words for "Established and Beautiful" after the nearby necropolis of Pepy I (*c.*2338–2298BCE) at Saqqara. In hieroglyphs it was written *mn–nfr/men-nefer*, using the signs for a game board, a water ripple, the lungs and trachea, a horned snake, a mouth, a pyramid and a city sign as determinative. The main deity of Memphis was the god Ptah, whose sacred precinct dominated the city during the years of the New Kingdom (1539–1075BCE). According to the creation myths developed in Memphis, Ptah was the creator god who brought the world into being.

Beyond Memphis lay Abydos in Upper Egypt, which was the most prominent burial ground of the early dynastic period. The name Abydos is derived from the ancient Egyptian "Abedju" and the Coptic "Ebot"; in hieroglyphs Abydos was written *3bḏw/ab-dew*, using a sign often identified as a chisel, the leg and foot, a mountain symbol and the town sign determinative. The local god, whose temple was situated in this province, was an early mortuary deity, the jackal-headed Khentamentiu. During the late Old Kingdom (2625–2130BCE), Abydos, which was associated with the death and resurrection of Osiris, rose to prominence as a major cult centre for the worship of that god. The area became particularly important to the New Kingdom kings, who wished to be identified with Osiris. The New Kingdom monarchs Sety I (*c.*1290–1279BCE) and Ramesses II (*c.*1279–1213BCE) built temples at Abydos. From the time of the Twelfth Dynasty (1938–1759BCE) onward, priests enacted annual Osirian mystery plays at Abydos, probably during the last month of the inundation season.

In the Eighteenth Dynasty (1539–1292BCE), Thebes in Upper Egypt was the home of the royal court and became a major religious centre. Of all ancient Egypt's sacred sites, Thebes, denoted *w3st/ooast*, is perhaps the best known – due to the discovery, close to the city's magificent temples, of the tombs of the New Kingdom kings and many of their priests and officials, which have revealed a great deal about the rituals and festivals in which these individuals participated. Thebes was the home of Egypt's national deity Amun, who during the New Kingdom was sovereign among the gods. The city was associated with the cult of the divine king, the royal son of Amun. The vast temple of Amun at Karnak was built in the heart of Thebes and connected to the smaller temple of Luxor, 1.8 miles

The central hypostyle hall and obelisks are clearly visible among the ruins of the huge temple at Karnak on the Theban East Bank. The complex, which was dedicated to the god Amun, was built by a succession of pharaohs.

(3km) to the south, by a processional pathway. On important feast days – such as the festival of Opet, which scholars believe was celebrated in the second month of the inundation – the cult statue of Amun was borne upriver within a boat shrine from Karnak to the Luxor temple, where the pharaoh took part in a rite designed to replenish his strength. The Egyptians understood the king's *ka* to be a divine essence that he shared with his royal ancestors. In the rite at Luxor temple, the king and his *ka* were reunited and his power was rejuvenated. Thebes was also the burial site of the New Kingdom rulers, whose tombs lined the Valley of the Kings, and whose royal consorts were buried nearby in the Valley of the Queens. The royal funerary temples were on the Theban West Bank, overlooking the Nile.

Hierakonpolis is the ancient Greek name for one of Egypt's most venerated sacred sites. The name means "the city of the falcon", for the site was associated with Horus, the falcon god whose head was decorated with two plumes. Hierakonpolis was known to the ancient Egyptians as Nekhen. Its modern name is Kom el-Ahmar, "the red mound". Here, along the edge of the desert, the extensive remains of predynastic settlements and cemeteries have been excavated. Egyptologists have found evidence that has helped scholars to reassess the architecture of primitive temples. The temples were designed with several rooms, and furnished with a sacred shrine; four large wooden pillars supported the facade. These structures are thought to be the prototypes of the New Kingdom temples.

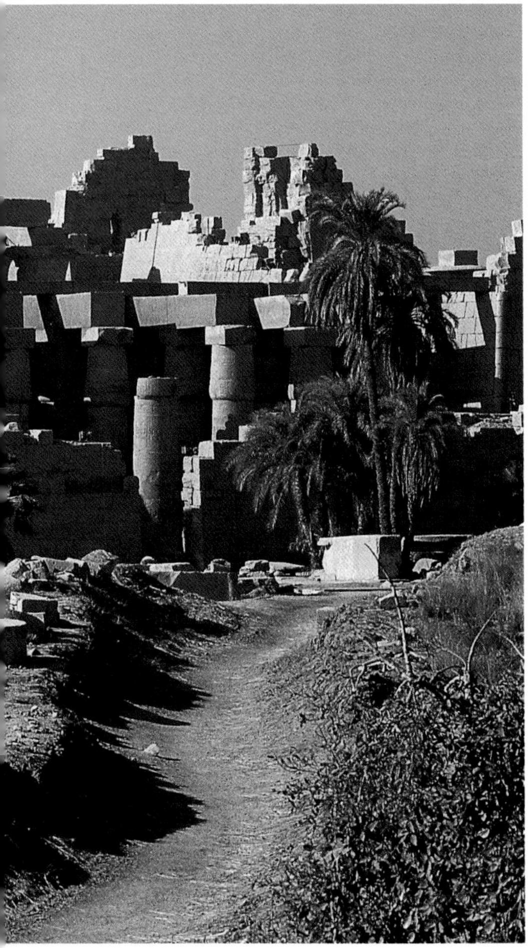

SACRED DIRECTIONS AND SITES

WEST *imnt/yo-ment* The word combines a bread loaf and double stroke with the emblem of the west surmounted by a feather. The setting of the sun in the west was held to indicate the descent of the sun god into the underworld. The ancient Egyptians buried their rulers on the West Bank of the Nile at Thebes in the Valley of the Kings.

KARNAK *ꜥIpt-swt/ipet-sut* The name of Karnak is written with a reed, a stool, two loaves, three thrones and a city determinative. The Karnak temple was known as "Most select of places".

EAST *i3bt/e-ah-bet* The emblem of the east, a foot and leg, a bread loaf and a double stroke combine to spell *i3bt*.

SACRED *wꜥb/warb* The adjective "sacred" is written with the symbol of a pouring vessel on legs and three water ripples.

DENDEREH *ꜥIwnt/ah-on-t* The word for this site was comprised of a column with tenon, plus a water ripple, a bread loaf and a city determinative sign. Dendereh in Upper Egypt was the site of a temple to the goddess Hathor.

PEOPLES BEYOND THE BLACK LAND

A carved relief on one of the giant statues of Ramesses II (c.1279–1213BCE) at Abu Simbel depicts Asiatic prisoners submitting to the pharaoh. The cartouche contains the prenomen (see pages 85 and 127) of Ramesses; reading from the left, the fragment of inscription reads: "...Egypt, his soldiers smite the foreign lands". The prisoners' hands are drawn behind their backs as in the symbol 𓀀 *that was used as a determinative for words associated with enemies or foreigners, including the word "Asiatic"* 𓂝𓅓𓀀 *ꜥ3m/amm.*

The Egyptians considered many non-Egyptians to be uncivilized, inferior peoples, the natural enemies of the "black land". However, some foreigners, including the Asiatics, enjoyed lucrative trade links with Egypt and even influenced Egyptian culture. The ancient Egyptian sign denoting "foreign country" 𓈉 *ḫ3st/hast* was composed of the hill-country sign, a bread loaf and a stroke.

From the end of the fourth millennium BCE onward, the Egyptians' ability to mobilize huge armies (see pages 122–123) enabled them to control their foreign interests and expand their empire, especially to the south. They used art to promote their supremacy by depicting their enemies being subjugated – foreigners were frequently shown grovelling before Pharaoh, begging for mercy. In royal iconography the king was frequently portrayed preparing to kill a group of foreigners, grasping them by their hair, a mace or sword raised above his head. Sometimes foreigners were referred to as the "nine bows", and images of them were painted on the base of royal sandals or on the pavements of palaces, where they would be symbolically trampled.

At the end of hieroglyphic words representing foreigners or foreign lands the Egyptians often added symbols that they associated with that country's inhabitants. Military elements appeared in many words relating to southerners (peoples whom the Egyptians regularly fought) – the signs for "Nubian" were typical examples. One version of "Nubian" 𓅓𓆓𓄿𓇌𓅱𓀀 *md3iw/med-jay* included a throwstick 𓌙, while another 𓈖𓎛𓋴𓇌𓀀 *nḥsy/n-has-y* was determined by

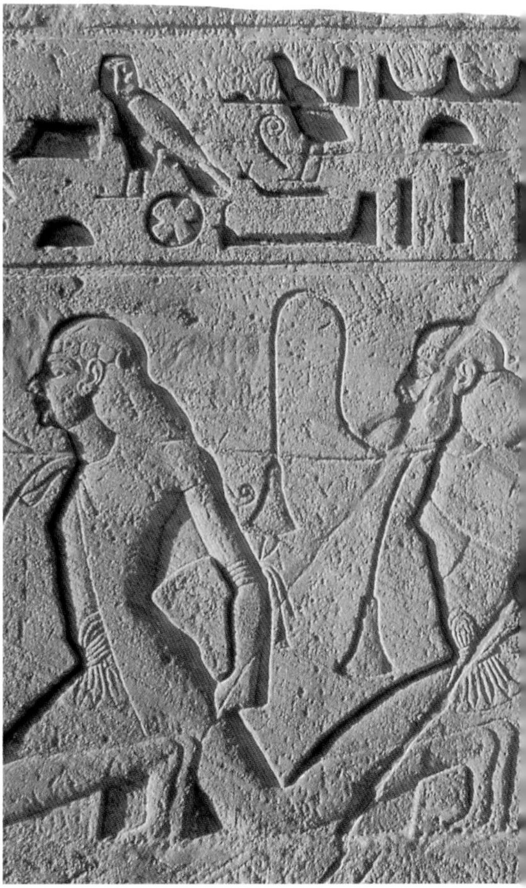

the sign of a bound captive. Another, 𓇋𓅱𓈖𓏏𓀀 *iwnt/oo–nt*, depicted both a bound prisoner and an archer's bow – the Egyptians regarded the Nubians as excellent bowmen. Immediately to the south of Egypt lay the Nubian kingdoms of Wawat and Kush. Egyptians often depicted this region's native peoples – whom they

described as "wretched" – with exaggerated facial features, short curly hair and earrings. By the New Kingdom (1539–1075BCE), the Egyptians had systematically colonized Nubia, and were exploiting it as a rich source of manpower, cattle, and gold. During the reign of Tuthmosis III (1479–1425BCE), the Egyptians expanded their control to the region of the Third Cataract of the Nile, deep in the heart of Kush, the hieroglyphic word for which, 𓎡𓄿𓈙𓈉 *k3š/kush*, included the hill country sign 𓈉.

Northwest of the Nile valley lay Libya, a land the Egyptians subjected to periodic punitive campaigns designed to establish territorial dominance. The Egyptians portrayed the Libyans, whom they frequently took as prisoners to serve in their army, as men wearing sidelocks of hair, pointed beards and head feathers.

Egyptian relations with the people of the Aegean region and the "Asiatics" were somewhat less warlike and were based essentially on trade. It is likely that the Egyptians traded by sea with the people of the Mediterranean region beginning at a very early date. Egyptian texts often describe a group of trading peoples called the "Keftiu", who probably originated on Crete. From the New Kingdom onward, the Egyptian king received paid tribute from the Aegean people. The Aegeans looked to Egypt for grain supplies, which they exchanged for commodities such as spices, oils and exotic goods.

Asia was separated from Egypt by 100 miles (160km) of desert. The barren territory of these "northern lands" provided the Egyptians with a causeway through Palestine to the important trading centres of Syria and Mesopotamia. Asiatics were generally reviled by the Egyptian population, often dismissed as "vile" or "wretched". Despite this popular antipathy, however, Egypt established various commercial ventures with Asiatics, some of whom migrated into Egypt. By the New Kingdom period, the hieroglyphic language was littered with West Semitic

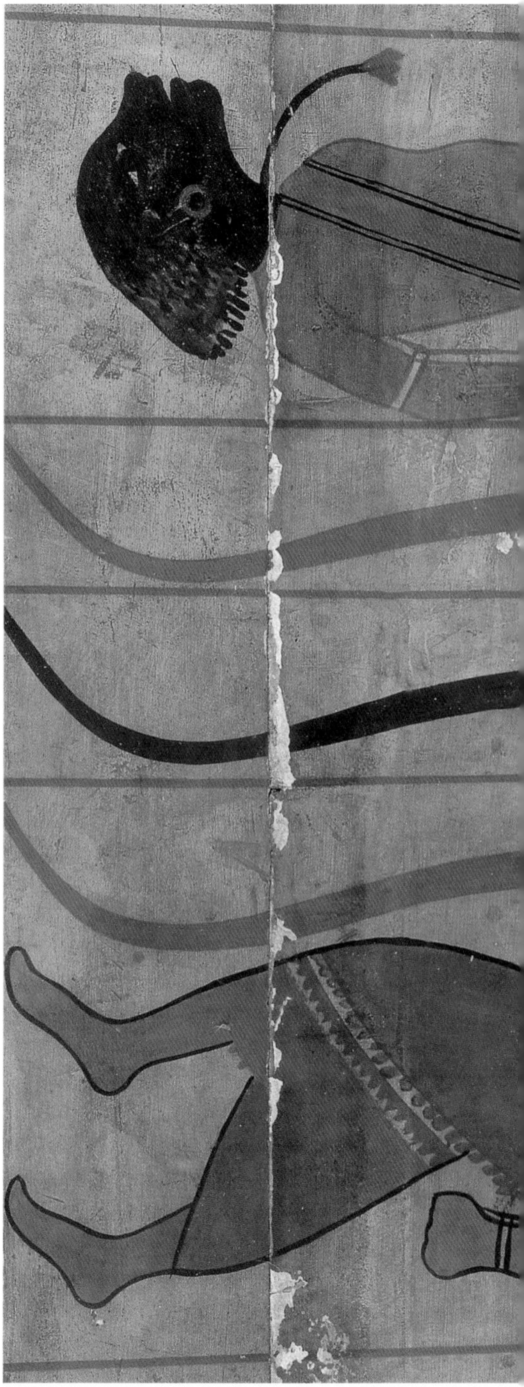

NEIGHBOURS, ENEMIES AND TRADERS

 NOMAD, FOREIGNER

šm3/shem-a The symbols of a pool of water, a sickle and a vulture spell *šm3*. The determinative is the image of a man carrying his belongings on his back.

 SYRIANS

fnḫw/fen-hekoo A horned snake, a water ripple, a placenta, a quail chick, a rope cord, and a seated figure with three strokes make up the word *fnḫw*, "Phonecians" or Syrians.

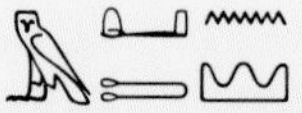 MITANNI

mṯn/m-cheten An owl, a hand with offering pot, a tethering rope, a water ripple and a hill country sign make up the word for Mitanni, a kingdom east of the Euphrates river.

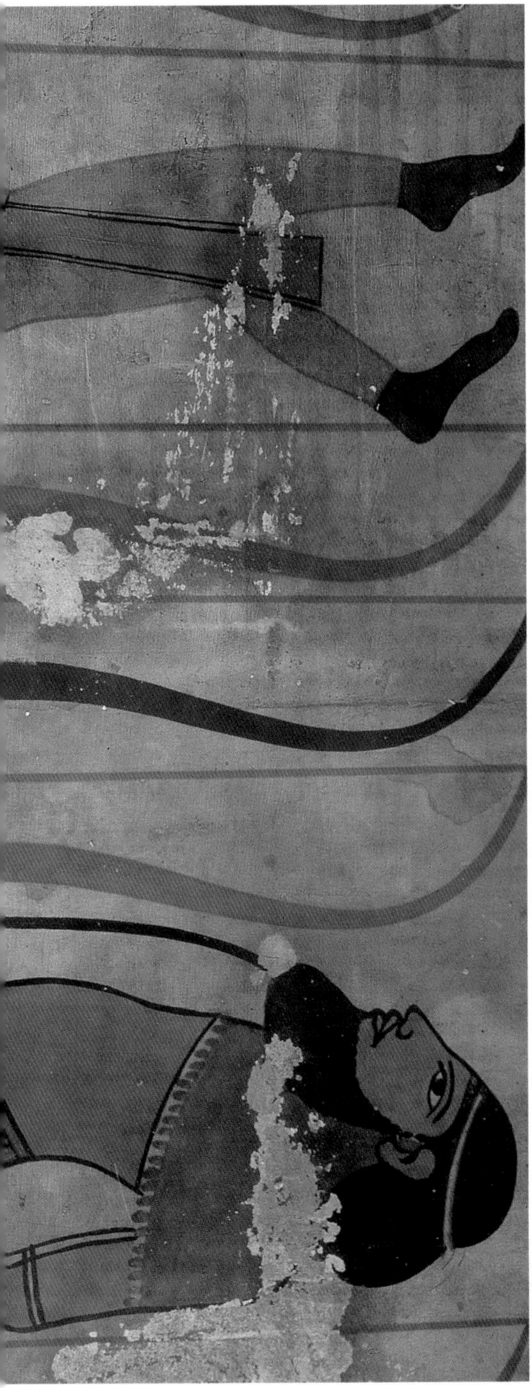

A detail from a tomb painting of the Greco-Roman period (332BCE–CE395) depicts two of the traditional foes of Egypt. The collective enemies of Egypt were known as the "Nine Bows".

aspects and infused with Asiatic expressions relating to trade and religion. Asiatic gods, such as the storm god Baal and the war deities Anath and Reshef, were adopted into the Egyptian pantheon. It was not unusual for an Asiatic – written in hieroglyphs either 𓂝𓄠𓀀 *ꜥ3m/eham* or as detailed in the caption on page 134 – to work and own property in Egypt. Some Asiatics even married Egyptians and overcame prejudice to rise to eminent positions in Egyptian society.

During the Fifteenth Dynasty (beginning 1630BCE), a contingent of Asiatics known as the Hyksos began to settle in northern Egypt. In just 100 years, the Hyksos took control of the Delta, and the Egyptians were subjected to a foreign rule that scarred the national psyche for generations to come. Following the expulsion of the Hyksos by Ahmose (1539–1514BCE), military strength was emphasized in Egyptian culture for 500 years.

The location of Punt, denoted by the hieroglyph 𓊪𓅱𓈖𓏏𓈉 *pwnt/punt*, remains a mystery, but the Egyptians are known to have traded with the Puntites from the Old Kingdom (2625–2130BCE) onward and seem to have navigated the route to Punt by boat along the Red Sea coast. Punt supplied Egypt with a range of exotic goods, including incense, ivory, ebony, gold and animal skins. Because it also produced luxury goods used by the clergy, Punt was often described as "gods' land".

CALCULATION & MEASUREMENT

The builders of the pyramids at Giza sought to defy time by building eternal tomb-mounuments to the kings Khufu (c.2585–2560BCE), Khafre (c.2555–2532BCE) and Menkaure (c.2532–2510BCE). The pyramids may have been meant to echo the form of the primeval mound from which, according to creation myths, the sun god had emerged (see pages 41–43).

Mathematical analysis played an important role in ancient Egypt, and the mathematicians of that time were capable of complex calculations. They used mathematics to create divisions for the day and year, and to define the astronomical cycles – and as so many aspects of measurement and time were linked with agriculture and the seasons, words connected to time were often represented by signs depicting images from the natural world.

TIME

The Egyptians were able to calculate time with a great deal of accuracy, dividing each day into twelve hours of light and dark. Every hour had its own name – the first hour of the day was called "the brilliant", while the last was known as "the period when Re restored himself to life" (see page 146). Priests were versed in these names, and the symbols for the night hours were sometimes placed on tomb walls to symbolize the sun's passage through the twelve zones of the underworld. The hours of the day were more rarely listed, although a stele in the British Museum records the exact hour of the birth of a child.

The passing of the hours could be marked by a water clock, which took the form of a perforated conical basin decorated with astronomical motifs. On the inner section, twelve vertical strips divided into equal sections were inscribed with the signs for life 𓋹 *ꜥnḫ/annk*, and duration 𓊽 *ḏd/djed*. The perforation was designed so that the water took exactly twelve hours to pass through, and periods of time were determined as the water dripped.

The sun symbol 𓇳 was the determinative for the words "day" 𓉔𓂋𓅱𓇳 *hrw/heroo* and the word "time" 𓂋𓎡𓇳 *rk/rek*. Rays of sunlight 𓇶 determine the verb "to rise" 𓅱𓃀𓈖𓇶 *wbn/weben*, while the sun rising over a mountain 𓈍 appeared with the bread loaf (*t*) and a single stroke in the word "horizon" 𓈍𓏏𓏤 *3ḫt/aket*. Phases of the night were usually marked by symbols of the moon 𓇹 or stars 𓇼.

THE SEASONS OF THE YEAR

The Egyptians regarded the year as an agricultural cycle rather than a period in which the Earth circumnavigated the sun. The word for "year" includes the symbol of a palm branch: rnpt/*renpit*. There were three seasons: inundation, which lasted roughly from mid-July to mid-November, was represented by *3ḫt/akhet*; winter, which lasted until mid-March, was spelled *prt/peret*; summer, the time of harvest, was written *šmw/shemu*. The beginning of a period could be shown as *tp/tep*, while the shoot could mark the seasons or define youth. The year began with the first day of akhet, marked by the first

1 five vertical strokes represent 5

2 three tens and seven ones represent 37

appearance of the star Sirius in the morning sky (on around 19 July in the modern calendar). The ebb and flow of the Nile played a crucial role in defining the three seasons. The Egyptians measured the height of the river using a Nilometer – inscribing an oval mark representing the mouth *r* on a stele or stone slab at the water's edge. By establishing the level of the water in this way, they could predict the extent of the flood, estimate the amount of land that would produce crops, and levy taxes accordingly.

The year was further divided into twelve months. The hieroglyphic word for "month" was *3bd/ahbed*. Each month was then divided into three weeks or decans of ten days, each corresponding with thirty-six divisions of the night sky – denoted by the positions of the constellations at certain hours of the night. Five extra days were added at the end of shemu or harvest season, bringing the total for each year to 365. These days were the birthdays of Osiris, Set, Isis, Nephthys and Horus, and were considered shadowy periods; they related to a time when the gods dwelt on earth and were classed as favourable, menacing or hostile. These influences were thought to affect the lives of citizens, so people would use amulets or avoid certain transactions on days regarded as unlucky. One quarter of a day was omitted from the year, so the calendar was miscalculated by one day every four years. In the Ptolemaic period (305BCE–CE30), the idea of the "leap year" familiar from modern usage was introduced from Babylonia.

Another periodic system of reckoning was linked to the festivals celebrated throughout the Egyptian year. These corresponded with seasonal and mythological events, and were often linked with cycles of the moon rather than the civil calendar. A text from the reign of Tuthmosis III (*c.*1479–1425BCE) found in the Karnak temple in Luxor lists fifty-four feast days in the year, while sixty were registered at Medinet Habu during the reign of Ramesses III (*c.*1187–1156BCE).

Dates could be recorded with reference to seasons and festivals, and they often appeared in royal inscriptions of a military nature. An example in the Annals of Tuthmosis III (see page 124) is: "Year 23, first (month) of the third season on the twenty-first day, the feast of the new moon, (corresponding to) the royal coronation, early in the morning." Inscriptions and records also dated events from the regnal year of the reigning king, which was denoted by *rnpt/ren-pet*.

Several numbers can be read in this copy of a wall painting from the Middle Kingdom (1980–1630BCE) tomb of a nobleman at Beni Hasan. The travellers (top) are Asiatic merchants arriving to trade eye paint in Upper Egypt.

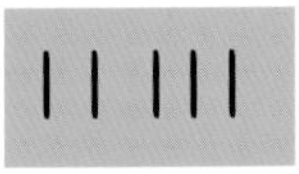

1 THE NUMBER FIVE WAS WRITTEN WITH FIVE VERTICAL STROKES (SEE PAGE 142). HERE IT APPEARS TO REFER TO THE LIVESTOCK.

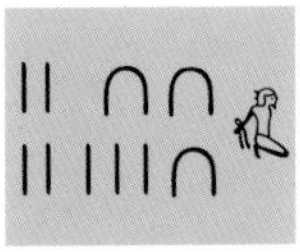

2 THREE TEN SIGN PLUS SEVEN STROKES REPRESENTS 37, HERE WRITTEN AT THE END OF A WORD DETERMINED BY THE SIGN, INDICATING "CAPTIVE" OR "FOREIGNER".

MATHEMATICS

Written in hieratic (see page 12), the calculations on this papyrus of c.1550BCE are largely concerned with working out the volume of a granary. Alongside a table for splitting an amount of grain into fractions, there is also a formula for calculating the area when squaring a circle.

From the early phases of Egyptian history, people needed to calculate figures for crop yields, land areas and the storage and measurement of grain. Calculation was also important to architectural and military practice – the cutting and transport of large blocks of stone for monumental statuary and architecture needed careful estimation and forward planning, while the scribes who oversaw military logistics needed to estimate the supply needs of large armies.

The detailed organization of labour, material supplies and product payment was important before money transactions were introduced in what scholars term the Late Period (664–332BCE). Taxation, tribute and booty lists were important elements of an economy founded on accounting. In several military scenes Egyptian scribes are shown counting the severed hands or phallic members of the enemy to estimate the number of dead.

Hieroglyphic writing used  *rẖt/rek-het* for "number" or "amount", while  *ip/epp* was the verb "to count". The Egyptians used a decimal system – counting in units, tens, hundeds and so on. Of the main numbers denoted by specific symbols, one was represented by , ten by , 100 by , 1,000 by , 10,000 by , 100,000 by  and 1,000,000 by . Other numbers were written as multiples of these single signs, the number of repetitions indicated either by writing multiple images of the sign or by placing a series of strike marks next to the single sign. The actual number was the sum of all these repetitions, The sign  *ʿš3/ashar* was used for "many".

Most mathematical tasks were done by adding and subtracting. The verb "to subtract" was written  *ḥbi/hebby*. Multiplication, for example, was achieved by adding a number to itself the required number of times – to multiply 10 x 4 an Egyptian would calculate 10+10+10+10. To divide, an Egyptian would subtract a number until an indivisible number remained. Egyptians used fractions but apart from 2/3 and 3/4, they did not use multiples of the single fraction unit – for example, 1/5 was used but 2/5, 3/5 and 4/5 were not used.

The sign  *ẖ3i/ha-ee* meant "to measure". The basic unit of measurement was the cubit, which was the average distance between the elbow and the fingertips. This distance was represented by  *mḥ/mha*, and is estimated at about 20 inches (50cm). A single cubit was subdivided into seven palms, each measuring about 3 inches (7.5cm) and represented by  *šsp/shesep*, while a palm could be

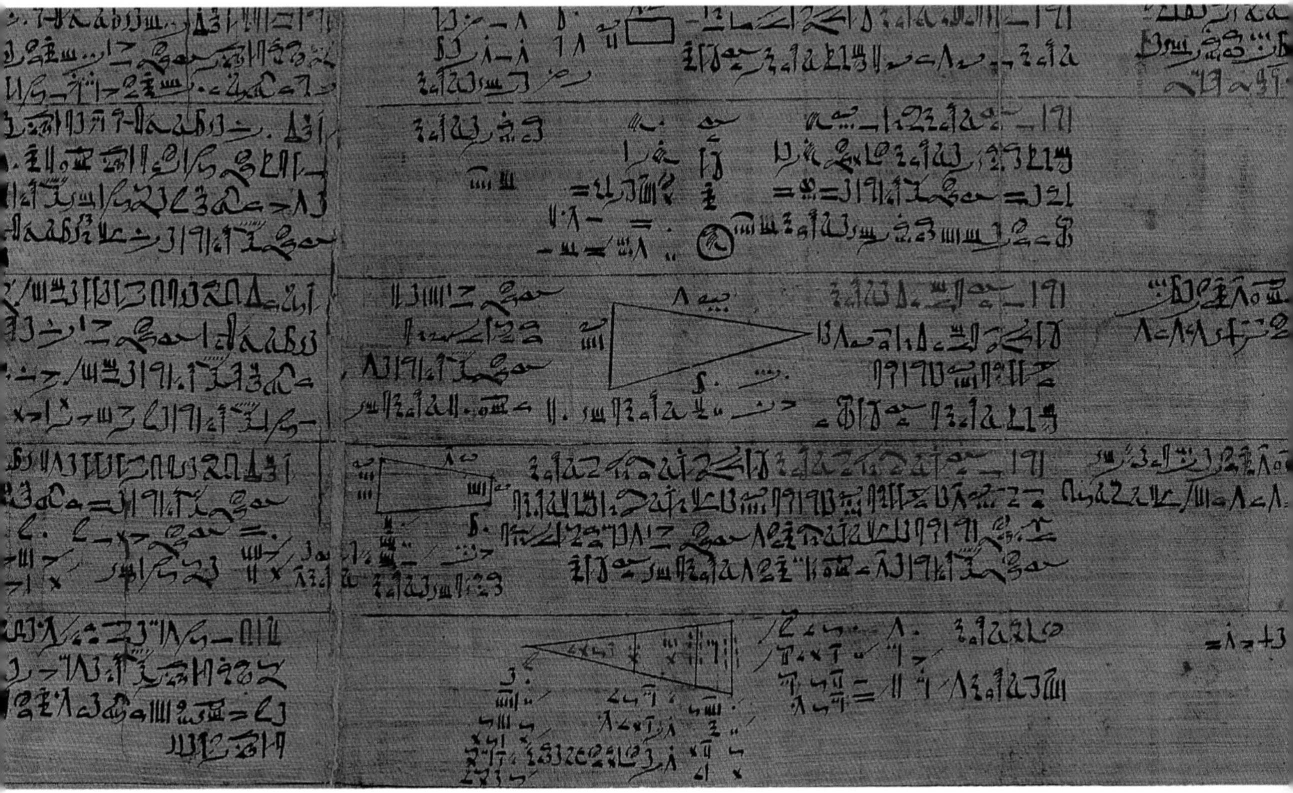

broken down into four finger widths – each one shown as 𓂭 *ḏbꜥ/jeb-ah*. An akhet (rod), which was represented by 𓐍𓏏𓏤 *ḫt/het*, equalled 100 cubits – around 55 yards (50 metres). The river-measure was a much larger unit, estimated at around 20,000 cubits – around 6.5 miles (10km) and represented by 𓇋𓏏𓂋𓅱𓈗 *itrw/eet-roo*. Agricultural areas were calculated in numbers of "setjet", a computation of 100 square cubits.

Liquids were generally measured by the hin, which was probably about one pint (0.6 litres). Grain measurements were based on the hekat, a unit of ten hin – 10 pints (6 litres). The standard measurement of weight was known as the deben, represented by 𓂧𓈖 *dbn/deben*; this is estimated at a little over two pounds (just under one kilogram) and was divided into ten units called qites, each represented by 𓈎𓏏 *kdt/kedet*.

2 Palm branch

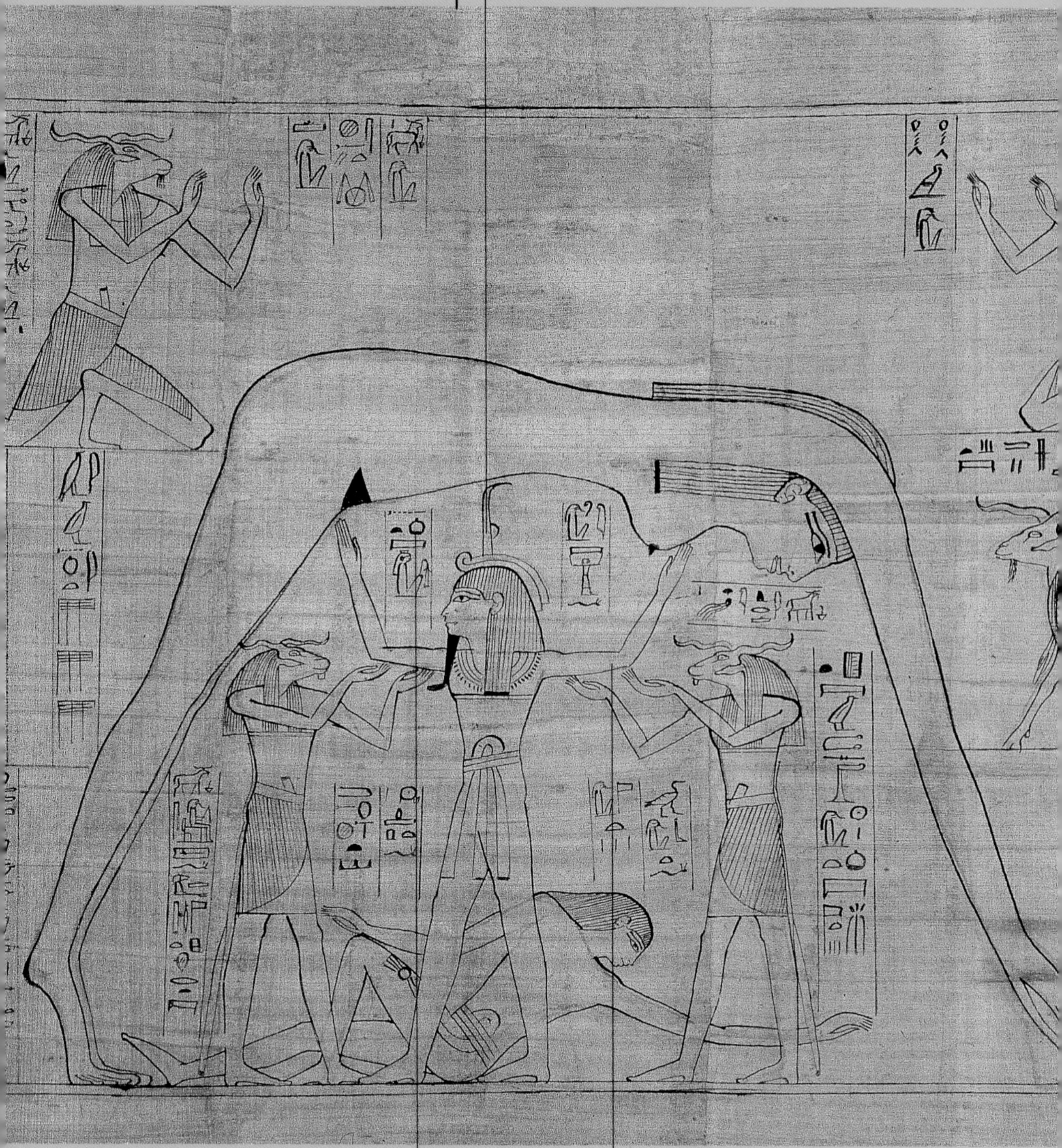

1 Nut

This figure can be compared to the hieroglyph of a worshipping male

CELESTIAL WORLDS

The Egyptians believed that the sky, like the Nile, was composed of water. By day, the sun sailed across the sky-ocean; by night the stars made the same journey while the gods and their entourage passed through the underworld and battled with the fearsome demons who lived there. To explain the origins of the world, the gods and humankind, the Egyptians developed a range of elaborate, diverse and sometimes contradictory creation stories.

CREATION MYTHS

Ancient Egyptian accounts of the creation of the world vary, but the concept of the "First Time" – the period leading up to the formation of the cosmos – was accepted in many traditions. Some creation myths identify this period with Nun, the waters of chaos from which a mound of earth arose to form the original island of creation (see page 41).

According to the creation myths developed at Heliopolis, the sun god Atum emerged as a child inside a lotus flower that grew from the primeval waters, representing the creation of order out of chaos. In his role as creator god, Atum had both male and female aspects, and spontaneously produced the first deities, Shu ("Air") and Tefnut ("Moisture"). They coupled to bring forth Geb ("Earth") and Nut ("Sky"), who in turn gave birth to Osiris and Isis, Seth and Nepthys the four gods who embodied creation, birth and sexuality (see page 41) for the ancient Egyptians.

Early myths suggest that Atum, in the form of a falcon, emerged from a divine egg. Theban theologists believed that Amun begot both gods and humans, while, according to the mythology of Memphis, Ptah created the gods from the "desire of his heart".

During the Middle Kingdom (2040–1640BCE), the Egyptians believed that humans were derived from the tears of the sun god. In another creation tale, the god Khnum created human beings from clay on his potter's wheel, and then breathed life into their bodies.

The god Shu separates Nut, the sky, from Geb, the earth, in a scene from the Book of the Dead. This version belonged to Nesitanebtashru, daughter of Pinudjem I, king of Upper Egypt.

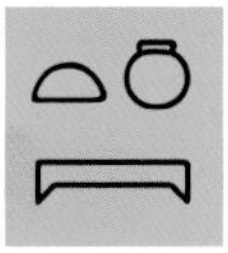

1 A DETAIL FROM JUST BENEATH THE STOMACH OF THE GODDESS SPELLS HER NAME - POT AND LOAF WITH SKY SYMBOL SPELL NWT/NUT.

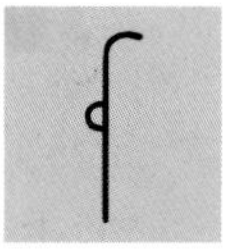

2 A DETAIL FROM THE HEAD OF THE FIGURE STANDING NEXT TO THE GODDESS'S NAME IS ſ, THE SYMBOL OF A PALM BRANCH, ASSOCIATED WITH HEALTHY GROWTH OR YOUTH.

DAY AND NIGHT

Solar themes permeate all aspects of Egyptian religion and culture. Dead kings were identified with the sun god Re, who triumphed over the forces of chaos each night and, reborn from the sky goddess *nwt/Nut*, cruised across the sky in a boat. The morning barque of the sun god was written *mꜥnḏt/man-jet*. The working day began as the sun rose, its rays sending a tangible lifeforce across the land, changing its colours and marking the daily behaviour of its inhabitants.

In later times, the sun had three manifestations: it was Khepri in the morning, Re at noon and Atum in the evening. This may relate to a vision of the sun as child in the morning, youth at midday and old man in the evening; in the Book of the Dead (see pages 74–75), it is described as the "aspect of the three". Khepri, sometimes written *hpr(i)*, was usually depicted as a scarab beetle *hpr*.

King Amenhotep III (*c*.1390–1353BCE) popularized worship of the Aten, a god personified by the disc of the sun *itn/aten*. His successor Amenhotep IV (*c*.1353–1336BCE) raised the Aten above all other gods. He changed his named to Akhenaten and moved his court to the new city of Akhetaten (Tel el-Amarna) in remote Middle Egypt, where the Aten was worshipped in courtyards open to the sun. By publicizing himself as the Aten's son, he elevated his divinity until it equalled that of the god himself; images may show the sun's rays tipped with hands, creating a tactile relationship between divinity and royal family.

The setting sun marked the descent of the sun god to the underworld *dw3t/do-att*, where he journeyed in a nocturnal barge, represented as *sktt/sket*. The night *grḥ/graha* was a shadowland, domain of the dead and rife with demonic elements.

The moon was linked with several deities: Thoth, Khonsu, Min, Shu and

HOURS OF LIGHT AND DARKNESS

DAY *hrw/heroo* A reed enclosure (*h*), a mouth (*r*) and a quail chick (*w*) spell *hrw*. The sun determines this word and morning (below).

MORNING *dw3t/do-att* Star, vulture and loaf spell *dw3t*.

SLEEP *ꜥꜥwy/eeoo* The eye determines "sleep", spelled with two arms, a quail chick and two strokes.

EVENING *mšrw/mesheroo* An owl with hand and arm, a pool of water above a mouth sign, the symbol of a lion at rest, a quail chick and a night sky depicted with a broken sceptre spell "evening".

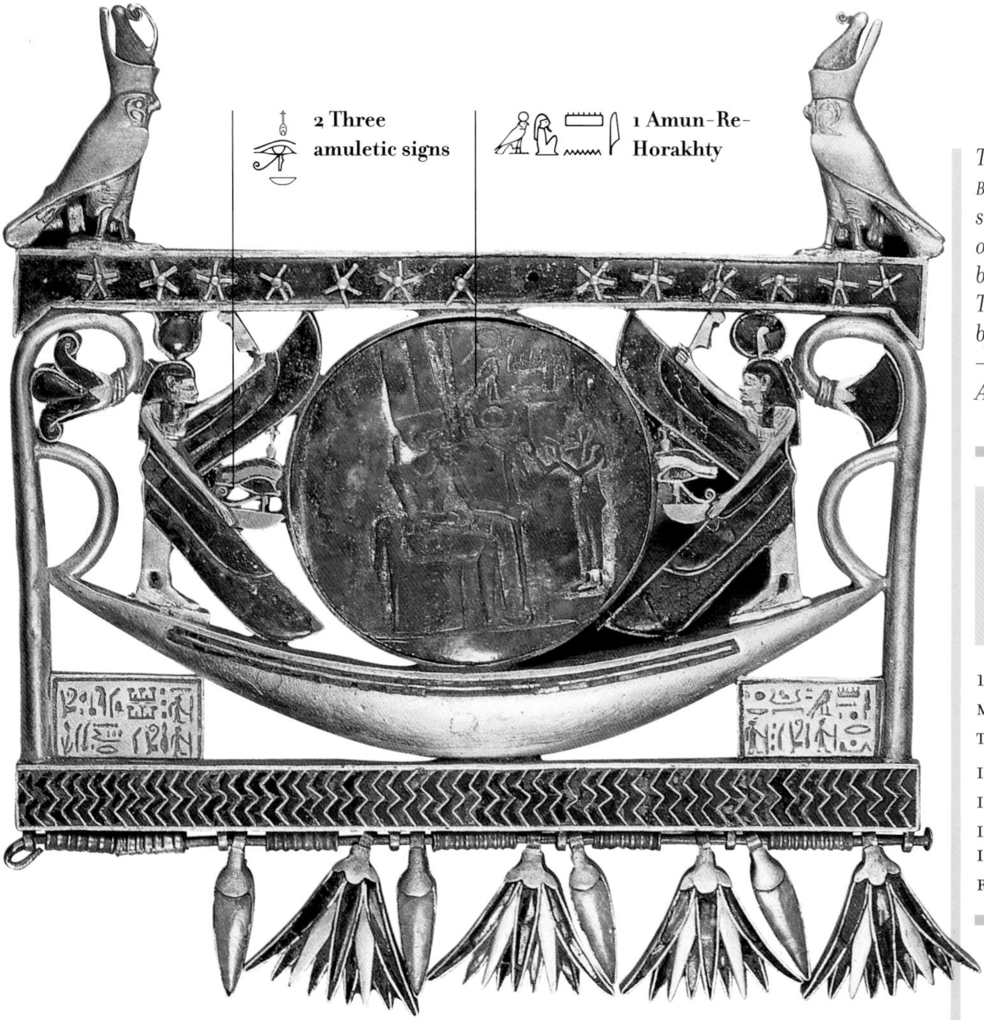

This tenth-century BCE *gold pendant shows a blue sun disc on a golden barque beneath a starry sky. The disc – protected by winged goddesses – shows Maat before Amun-Re-Horakhty.*

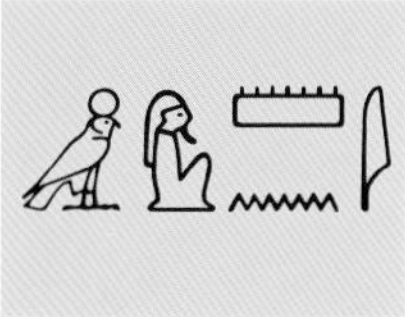

1 i/EE, MN/ MEN, N/EN MAKE THE NAME OF AMUN; IS THE DETERMINATIVE INDICATING THAT IT IS A GOD'S NAME. IS Rʿ-ḤR-3ḪTY/ RAY-HOR-AKTY).

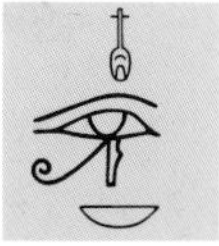

2 THESE THREE SIGNS WERE WORN AS AMULETS – NFR/ NEFER ("GOOD"); THE EYE OF HORUS WḎ3T/WEDJAT (A PROTECTIVE AMULET); AND NB/NEB ("EVERYTHING").

Khnum. The moon and sun together were associated with the eyes of Horus and the lunar (left) eye became known as the *wd3t/wedjat* or the "sound eye" after Seth damaged it and Thoth restored it to health (see also pages 30–33).

Lector priests (see pages 112–114) were skilled in interpreting dreams. The Egyptians believed that the gods and the dead sent messages by way of dreams, and patients hoping to receive healing dreams patronized sanctuaries in the temple precincts; some people hired magicians to send demons into the dreams of their enemies. Tuthmosis IV (*c*.1400–1390BCE) even received a vision from the sphinx, which promised to place him on Egypt's throne if he cleared its edifice of sand.

THE WATERS OF HEAVEN

A carving from the Ptolemaic era (323–30BCE) temple of Hathor at Dendereh depicts the beings believed to inhabit the heavens. The modern zodiac derives from the Egyptian view of the night sky.

1 A DETAIL FROM THE RIGHT OF THE PICTURE SHOWS JꜥH/JAR, THE WORD FOR "MOON". THOTH, GOD OF WISDOM AND OF SCRIBES, WAS LINKED TO THE MOON.

2 A DETAIL (BOTTOM LEFT) SHOWS SB3/SABA, THE WORD FOR "STAR". IN THE PYRAMID TEXTS, THE STARS WERE IDENTIFIED WITH THE SOULS OF THE DECEASED IN THE FIELD OF OFFERINGS.

The Egyptians saw the sky as a celestial ocean, a reiteration of the Nile encircling the Earth, while the "duat" or underworld *d3t/do-att* was the womb of the sky goddess Nut. At the rim of the night sky was the Field of Reeds or Field of Offerings, where the circumpolar stars never set, and early Old Kingdom (2625–2130BCE) pyramids pointed in this direction, perhaps linking the dead to the "imperishable ones".

Records dating to the New Kingdom (1539–1075BCE) refer to five planets – Jupiter, Mercury, Venus, Saturn and Mars – and to constellations associated with the gods. The Pyramid Texts (see pages 70–71) also mention "the beaten path of stars" or Milky Way. As agriculturists, the Egyptians used star maps to indicate the changing seasons. The dogstar Sirius was most important: associated with Isis, whose tears caused the river to flood, it reached its high point around 19 July, heralding the onset of the inundation (see pages 140–141). Maps on temple ceilings often showed gold stars on an azure sky, while basalt floors mimicked the fertile earth. In the tomb of Ramesses IV (*c.*1156–1150BCE), the sun appears cruising though the body of Nut, the sky.

MAPPING THE STARS

HEAVEN *ḥrt/hurt* A frontal view of a face (*hr*), a mouth (*r*) and a loaf (*t*) spell *ḥrt*; the sky sign is the determinative.

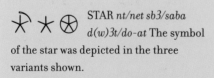

STAR *nt/net sb3/saba d(w)3t/do-at* The symbol of the star was depicted in the three variants shown.

HALF-MONTH FESTIVAL *nt/net* A combination of half the sign for a crescent moon and a star sign links with a water ripple, a loaf and an alabaster purification basin in *nt/net*, the word for "half-month festival".

MONTH *3bd/abed* Words associated with the passing of time often include star signs. Here the sign sits beneath the crescent moon.

ISLAND *iw/yo* The stars were regarded as islands in the celestial waters. A section of land, a vegetation sign and a stroke spell *iw*.

2 Star ✳

1 Crescent moon

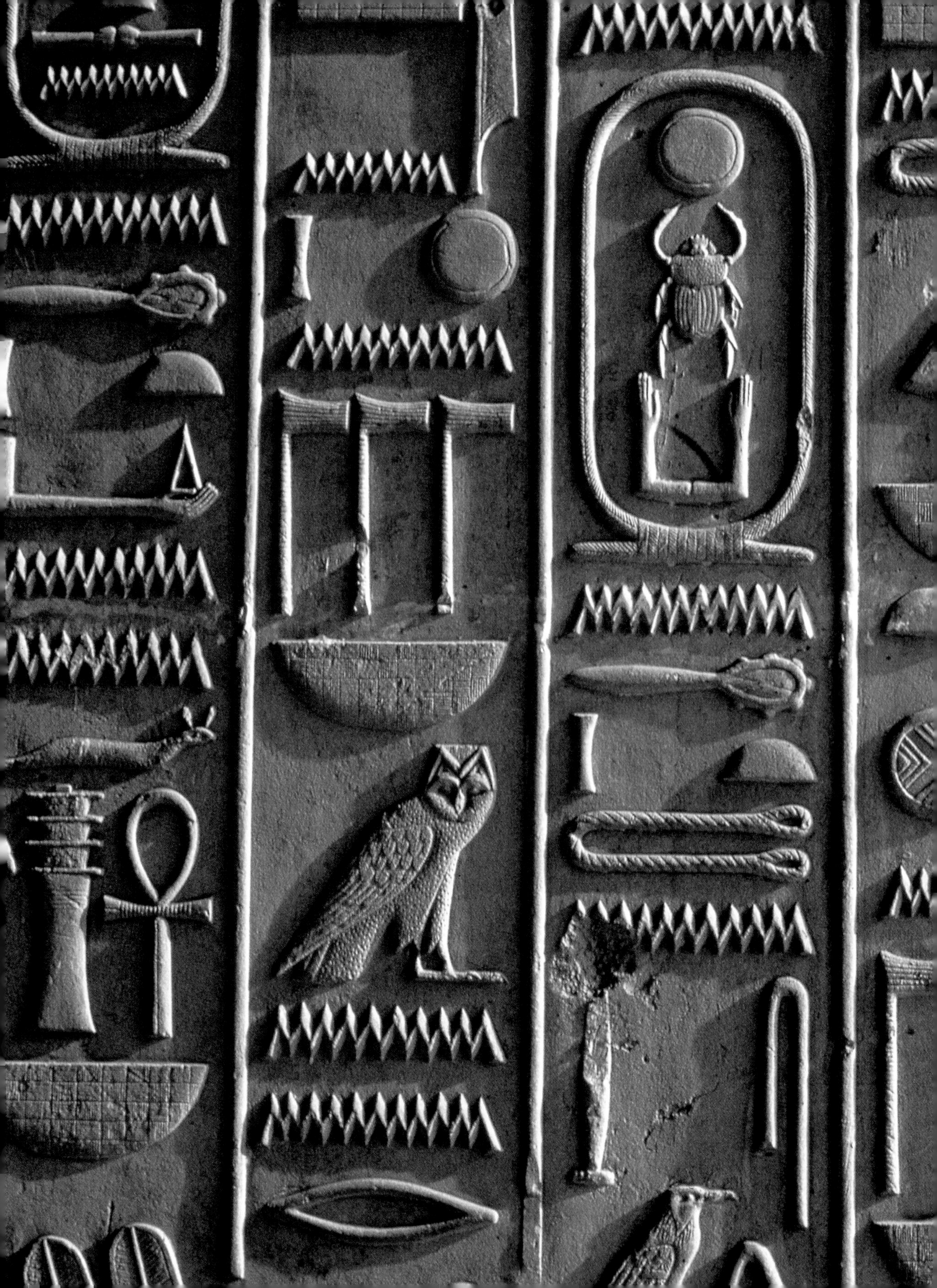

CHAPTER FIVE

REFERENCE FILE

In the hieroglyphic system of writing, ancient Egyptian scribes had a flexible tool that enabled them to make lasting expression of complex thought. This reference section provides a basic introduction to the grammar of hieroglyphic writing and a comprehensive, easily used index of the signs used in this book.

The cartouche of Senwosret I (c.1919–1875BCE) is repeated in this Karnak inscription: it means Kheper-ka-Re ("the ka of Re comes into being").

THE GRAMMAR OF HIEROGLYPHS

Once we have familiarized ourselves with the hieroglyphic alphabet (see pages 22–23) and the use of determinative signs (see pages 24–25), we are ready to investigate the grammar of hieroglyphs. Egyptian grammar is a complex subject, still much debated among academic specialists, but by acquiring a little basic knowledge and following a few simple guidelines, it is possible to derive a greater understanding and pleasure from reading the hieroglyphs on monuments, in tomb paintings and on other artefacts.

The first hieroglyphic texts were written in the language that scholars call Old Egyptian, which originated in the Old Kingdom (2700–2200BCE). However, most examples given in this book are of Middle Egyptian. Found in written texts from the period *c*.2200–*c*.1800BCE, Middle Egyptian is generally regarded as the classical period of the language and the easiest to master (see also page 13).

The following pages provide a selective beginners' guide to the grammar of Middle Egyptian hieroglyphs. They include sections on nouns, adjectives, verbs, linking words, prepositions, pronouns, word order, negatives and sentences without verbs as well as a further examination of the alphabet (see also pages 22–23). The section concludes with details of how to read kings' titles and dates. In these pages, to make it easier to match hieroglyphs with their English translations, only the transliteration is given and not the pronunciation (see pages 20–21). For example, with "brother" *sn/sen* only the transliteration *sn* is given (see below).

Nouns

Masculine and Feminine

Masculine nouns have no suffixes to indicate gender. Feminine nouns end in *t*. For example:

sn "brother"
snt "sister".

Masculine nouns may end with a determinative that shows a connection to men or to male activities. For example:

it "father"
b3k "man servant"
rḫty "washerman".

Here the symbol is determinative of a word to do with a man. In *h3y* "husband", the phallus sign fulfils a similar determinative function.

Sometimes feminine nouns include the determinative to indicate that the word is associated with a woman or a woman's task. Examples include:

 *mwt* "mother"
 *s3t* "daughter".

These both contain two female determinatives – the  and the  signs.

Words that are neither feminine nor masculine take a feminine ending. Examples include the names of countries and towns:

 *kmt* the name for Egypt (the "black land", see page 126)
 *ˁIpt-swt* Karnak
 *w3st* Thebes
 *niwt* "city".

All four also use the generic determinative , which indicates that the word is the name of a town, village or country.

SINGULAR, PLURAL AND DUAL

Middle Egyptian distinguishes between three types of number: singular, plural and dual. The plural ending is  *w* for masculine nouns and  *wt* for feminine nouns:

 *sn* "brother" becomes
 *snw* "brothers";
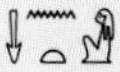 *snt* "sister" becomes
 *snwt* "sisters".

In both these words three strokes are added to reinforce the message that this is a plural word (see below).

The dual is used for pairs. Masculine pairs end in ; feminine pairs end in :

 *sn* "brother" becomes
 *snwy* "a pair of brothers";
 *snt* "sister" becomes
 *snty* "a pair of sisters".

In each case the determinative is doubled.

Occasionally, an ideogram in a word is repeated to indicate plural:

 *ḥk3* "magic" becomes
 *ḥk3w* "magical spells";
 *nṯr* "god" becomes
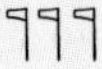 *nṯrw* "gods" or
 *nṯrwy* "a pair of gods".

The phonetic spelling of the words (see pages 20–21) is often used together with the repeating ideograms, for example  *srw* "officials", where  spells *sr* "official",  *w* indicates a masculine plural noun and the three repeated ideograms  reinforce the idea of plural number. Here, the repeated ideogram is the generic determinative (see page 24) for words associated with officialdom and public authority. More often, three strokes beneath or at the side of the word indicates a plural, making it unnecessary to repeat the ideogram. For example:

nṯr "god" becomes
nṯrw "gods";
pr "house" becomes
prw "houses".

VERBS

In Egyptian the verb stem forms the basis on to which tense signs are added. For the beginner it is enough to recognize the past and present tenses. For example:

sḏm-f "He hears"
sḏm n-f "He heard".

The past tense is denoted by the *n* sign that directly follows the verb stem.

ADJECTIVES

Adjectives generally follow nouns – for example "good son" would be written:

s3 "son" *nfr* "good".

Adjectives also agree with the gender of the noun they describe.

"Good man" is written:
s "man" *nfr* "good";
"Good woman" is written:
st "woman" *nfrt* "good".
"Excellent brother" is written:
sn "brother" *ikr* "excellent";
"Excellent sister" is written:
snt "sister" *ikrt* "excellent".

In each of these cases the bread loaf sign is added to the adjective to make it agree with the feminine noun.

Adjectives can be used independently of a noun, and take on something of the character of a noun. In this case they are written with a determinative that makes the meaning clear. For example: *nfrt* means "the beautiful woman", and is written "the beautiful one (woman)" – with the determinative sign indicating that the beautiful one is a woman and the bread loaf sign *t* re-emphasizing that she is female. The signs, transliterated as *nfr*, can mean "beautiful" or "good".

LINKING WORDS

Hieroglyphic writing does not use the definite article "the" or the indefinite article "a". According to context, the word chapel *r-pr* can be translated "the chapel", "a chapel" or "chapel". There is no hieroglyphic word for "and" – when scribes wanted to link two things or people they simply juxtaposed them:

sn snt "brother and sister"
snw snwt "brothers and sisters".

When the ancient Egyptians wanted to express a possessive relation between two nouns, they placed the two nouns next to each other, for example:

ḥwt-nṯr "house of God" or "temple"
imy-r pr "overseer of the house" or "steward". 

PREPOSITIONS

In hieroglyphic writing, prepositions consist either of single words (known as simple prepositions) or of more than one word (compound prepositions). A preposition is always followed immediately by the noun it governs.

These are the main prepositions:

m "in", "with", "from", "as"
r "as to", "to", "toward"
n "to" (a person)
ḥr "upon", "on"
ẖr "under"
ḫr "with", "near"
in "by"
ḥnꜥ "together with".

PRONOUNS

Three types of pronoun are commonly used in hieroglyphic writing: suffix, dependent and independent.

Suffix pronouns are so called because they are used as a suffix ending to nouns, prepositions and verbs. They must follow and be attached to a preceding word. They are used when a person performs an action ("*he* found a fruit") and to show possession ("*his* tomb").

The main suffix pronouns are:

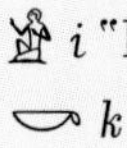

i "I", "me", "my"
k "you", "your" (singular masculine)
ṯ "you", "your" (singular feminine)
f "he", "him", "his", "it", "its" 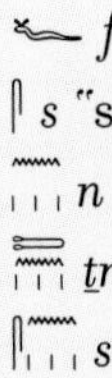
s "she", "her", "hers", "it", "its"
n "we", "us", "our"
ṯn "you", "your" (plural)
sn "they", "them", "their".

Dependent pronouns denote the object of an action – "hitting *him*". Unlike suffix pronouns, they do not have to be attached to a preceding word – they can stand alone. They never occur as the first word in a sentence.

The dependent pronouns are:

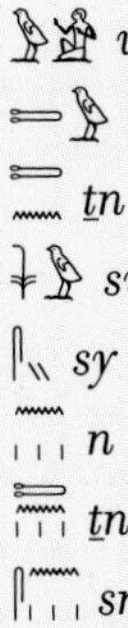

wi "I", "me"
ṯw "you", "your" (masculine)
ṯn "you", "your" (feminine)
sw "he", "him", "it"
sy "she", "her", "it"
n "we", "us"
ṯn "you" (plural)
sn "they", "them".

Independent pronouns always come first in the sentence. Their use gives added emphasis to the pronoun – "You saw it!". The independent pronouns are:

ink "I"
ntk "you" (masculine)
ntṯ "you" (feminine)
ntf "he", "it"
nts "she", "it"
inn "we"
nttn "you" (plural)
ntsn "they".

WORD ORDER

The order of words in Egyptian sentences determines whether a noun is the subject or object of the verb – whether the three words "I/me", "hit" and "he/him" mean "I hit him" or "he hits me". The normal order is verb, noun-subject, noun-object. For example:

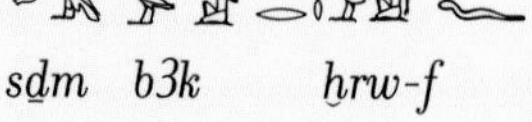

sḏm b3k ẖrw-f
"hears" (*sḏm*) "the servant" (*b3k*) "voice" (*ẖrw*) "his" (*f*) – "the servant hears his voice".

When the sentence contains an adverb or adverbial phrase, the order is verb, noun-subject, noun-object, adverb/adverbial phrase. For example:

m33 s rꜥ m pt
"saw" (*m33*) "the man" (*s*) "the sun" (*rꜥ*) "in" (*m*) "the sky" (*pt*) – "the man saw the sun in the sky".

When the object of the sentence is a dependent pronoun (see page 155) and the subject is a noun, the word order changes as follows: verb, object (pronoun), subject (noun), adverb or adverbial phrase. "The man found him in Egypt" is written:

gm sw s m kmt
"found" (*gm*) "him" (*sw*) "the man" (*s*) "in" (*m*) "Egypt" (*kmt*).

Word order also changes in sentences involving an indirect object. Then the sentence follows the order verb, subject, object, indirect object, adverb or adverbial phrase. For example, "the scribe gives praise to the god in the chapel" is written in the following order in English: subject ("the scribe"), verb ("gives"), object ("praise"), indirect object in dative case ("to the god"), adverbial phrase ("in the chapel"). In hieroglyphs it follows the order verb ("gives") subject ("the scribe"), object ("praise"), indirect object ("to the god") adverbial phrase ("in the chapel"):

rdi sš hnw n ntr m rpr

"gives" (*rdi*) "the scribe" (*sš*) "praise" (*hnw*) "to" (*n*) "the god" (*ntr*) "in" (*m*) "the chapel" (*r-pr*).

When the indirect object is a pronoun the noun must not precede the pronoun and the dependent pronoun is never written before the suffix pronoun (see page 155). For example, the English sentence "the man gives the bread to you" would be written by ancient Egyptians "gives to you the man bread":

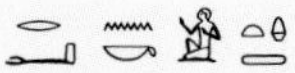

rdi n-k s t

"gives" (*rdi*) "to you" (*n-k*) "the man" (*s*) "bread" (*t*).

NEGATIVES

When the ancient Egyptians wished to express a negative they commonly used two forms: *n* and *nn*. appears in sentences in the past tense and negates the narrative verb, whereas *nn* usually has a future meaning. In both past- and future-tense sentences the negative word always appears before the verb at the beginning of the sentence:

n sḏm-f

"He did not hear";

nn sḏm-f

"He will not hear".

However, if the negative is in the present tense *n* is placed after the verb if the verb is followed by a suffix pronoun, as in this example:

sḏm n n-f

"He does not hear".

When verbs are negated the function of the sign is reversed. Here it denotes the present tense, rather than the past tense (see page 154).

SENTENCES WITHOUT VERBS

Some sentences in hieroglyphic writing omit the verb. The missing verb is often "to be" and the sentences usually remain easily comprehensible. For example:

rꜥ m pt

is translated "sun in sky", probably meaning "the sun [is/was] in the sky". It can be difficult to distinguish between past, present and future, but the tenses can often be deduced from the context in which the sentence appears. For example, hieroglyphs that indicate the future usually feature on monuments of the dead such as stele and are concerned with ensuring that the deceased will be remembered by the living.

The Alphabet

Ancient Egyptian used a basic alphabet of 24 single-consonant letters (see pages 22–23). In addition, the language made use of a number of signs that represented two consonants (biliteral signs) and three consonants (triliteral signs). Some of these were given on pages 22–23. A fuller list follows here:

Selected biliteral signs, with pronunciations:

ir/er
ꜥ3/aa
w3/wa
b3/ba
p3/pa
m3/ma
ḥ3/ha
ḫ3/kha
ẖ3/ha
s3/sa
š3/sha
k3/ka
t3/ta
ṯ3/cha
mn/men
wn/wen
ḫn/hen
šn/shen
in/in
wn/wen
nn/nen
im/im
ḥm/hem
km/kem
gm/gem
tm/tem
wp/wep
kp/kep
mi/mee
ti/tee
wꜥ/wa
hꜥ/ha
3w/ow
nw/noo
hw/hoo
sw/soo
iw/yoo
ḫw/khoo
ḏw/dja
mw/moo
rw/roo
sw/soo
3b/ab
pr/pair
or *mr/mer*
ḥr/her
wr/wer
ḏr/der
mḥ/meh
nḥ/neh
is/iss
ns/ness

ḥs/hess
šs/sess
ꜥḳ/ak
sk/sek
mt/met
mt/moot
ḫt/khet
šd/sed
ḳd/ked
ḏd/djed
ꜥḏ/adj
wḏ/wedj
nḏ/nedj
ḥḏ/hedj.

Selected triliteral consonants

Three-consonant signs are not as widely used as two-consonant signs and do not need to be listed exhaustively. Here are a few common examples:

ḫpr/kheper
nfr/nefer
nṯr/netjer
ꜥnḫ/ankh
wsr/woser
hrw/heroo.

Royal Epithets

The following are commonly used titles given to the king in inscriptions:

nṯr-nfr
"good god";

nb nswt t3wy
"lord of the two lands";

nsw bit
"king of Upper and Lower Egypt".

These titles often precede the king's fourth name or prenomen, which is contained in a cartouche (see pages 82–85). The title *s3-Rꜥ* "son of Re" often precedes the king's fifth name or prenomen, also contained in a cartouche. The titles *di ꜥnḫ* "given life" and *di ꜥnḫ ḏt* "given life eternally" are often written after the names. Other words that appear frequently in texts associated with kingship include:

ḥm "majesty"
iti "sovereign"
bity "king of Lower Egypt"
ni-swt "kingship"
pr-ꜥ3 "pharaoh".

Dates

The following dates and seasonal names appear frequently in inscriptions:

rnpt "year"
3bd "month"
tr "season"
i3ḫi "inundation"
šmw "summer"
prt "winter".

SAMPLE TRANSLATIONS

A selection of sentences and phrases with transliterations and English translations provides an opportunity to practise recognition of hieroglyphs in everyday usage and (opposite) in a typical royal inscription naming Amenemhet III (*c*.1818–1772BCE). By working out which signs correspond to which English word, you will become familiar not only with common vocabulary but also with hieroglyphic word order and sentence structure. Examples of signs can be found in the Sign Index on pages 166–71.

rc *m* *pt*
ray em pet
"The sun is in the sky"

3pd *ḥr* *mw*
aped her moo
"The bird is on the water"

s *m* *sš*
es em sesh
"The man is [as] a scribe"

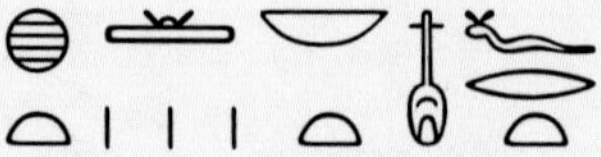

ḫt *nbt* *nfrt*
heket nebet nefert
"All good things"

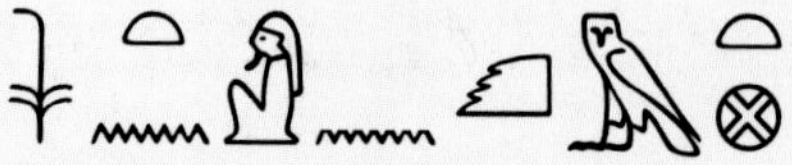

nsw *n* *kmt*
nesoo en kemet
"The king of Egypt"

ḥmwt *nt* *sr*
hemet-oo net ser
"The wives of the chief"

ḥmt *m* *pr*
hemet em pair
"The woman is in the house"

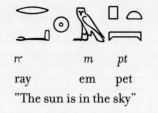

nn *sḏm-f*
nen sed-jem-ef
"He shall not hear"

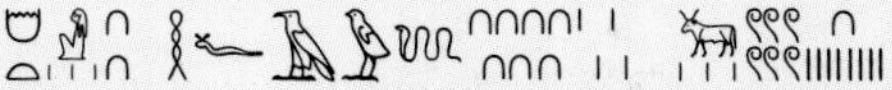

ḥmwt 20 ḥf3w 74 iḥw 618

hamoot 20 hefoo 74 eehoo 618

"20 women, 74 snakes and 618 cattle"

mri n it- f wr n mwt-f sfn

merry en eat-ef wier en moot-ef sef-en

"Beloved by his father, treasured by [important to] his gentle mother"

rḫ ib nb-f

rech eb neb-ef

"Knowing the desire of his lord"

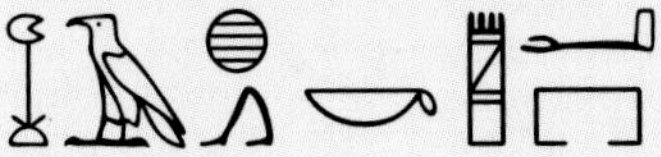

ḥ3ḥ- k ꜥḥ

hek-ah-hek ek ah

"You must make haste to the palace"

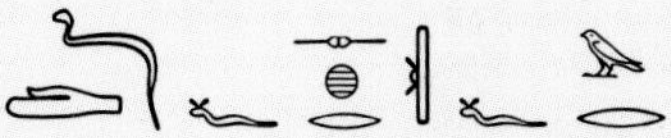

ḏd-f sẖr-f wr

jed-ef seker-ef wier

"He recited his important plan"

prt- i

peret- ee

"I had come forth"

imi n ḳnd rmṯ

eemee en kend rem-chet

"Let not mankind be angry"

m snḏ

em sen-jay

"Do not worry!"

A ROYAL INSCRIPTION

rnpt sp 19 ḥr ḥm n nṯr nfr nb t3wy n-m3ꜥt-Rꜥ, s3-Rꜥ, imn-m-ḥ3t

ren-pet sep 19 hek-air hem en netcher nefer neb tar-way en maht-Ray, sar Ray, amun-em-het

"Year 19 of [the reign of] the majesty of the good god, lord of the two lands Nema're' son of Re', Amenemhet III"

sḫpr-ni ḫt

s-heper-nenny heket

"I created fire"

ḥtp n nṯr m ḫnt-š

hetep-en netcher em hek-ent-esh

"The god rested in the garden"

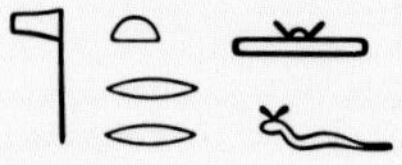

nṯrr-f

netcher-ef

"He is divine"

rḫ n- k tḫ-f

rek en- ek t-hek-ef

"You knew he was drunk"

sḫ sn

sha sen

"They are deaf"

sw(r)i- f

swery- ef

"He drinks"

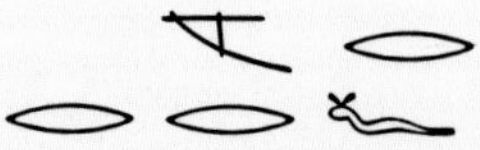

r mrr-f

r mer-ef

"As he deserves"/"As he wishes"

ḥrrt nbt nfrt

herret nebet nefert

"Every beautiful flower"

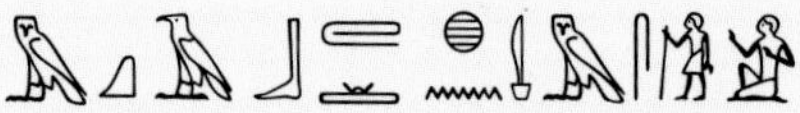

m k3b ḫnms

em kab hek-en-mess

"In the company of friends"

ḥmt m kmt

hemet em kemet

"A woman of Egypt"/"Egyptian woman"

in *mrwt* *ḥtpn*

een merr-oot hetep-en

"Through love of forgiveness"

ink *sḥwr* *nb-f*

enk shweer neb-ef

"I am one cursed by his lord"

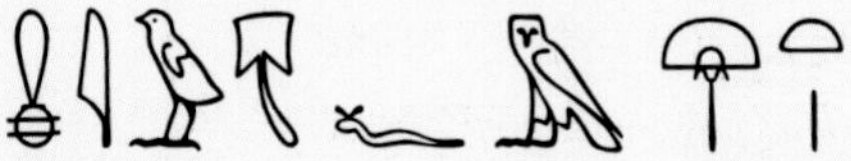

miw- *f* *m* *šwt*

me-ow- ef em shewt

"His cat is in the shade"

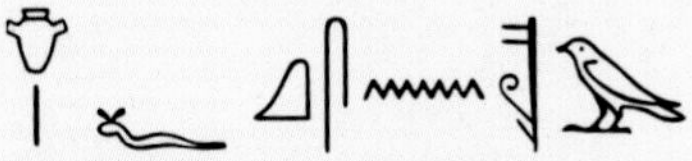

ib- *f* *ḳsn*

ib- ef kesen

"His heart is disagreeable"

iḫ *tmi* *iš3-r*

yo-hek temmy ah-shar

"There, I'll not chatter"

dpt *ḥr* *mw*

depet her moo

"The boat is on the water"

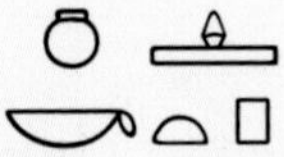

ink *ḥtp*

enk hetep

"I am content"

in *mri-k* *ḥmt-k*

yo merry-ek hemet-ek

"Do you love your wife?"

mnmnt *nbt* *ibw-sn* *rmi*

mement nebet iboo-sen remi

"All cattle, their hearts weep"

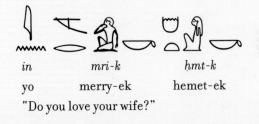

hy *n-k*

hay n-ek

"Hail to you"

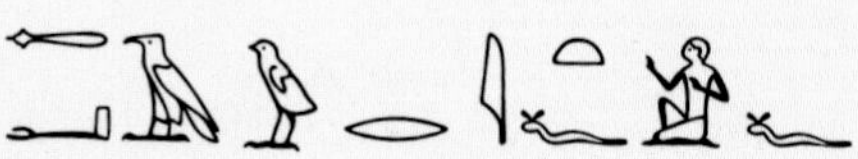

ꜥ3 r it- f
ah ah it- ef
"Greater than his father"

itrw ꜥš3
it-roo ash–ar
"Many rivers"

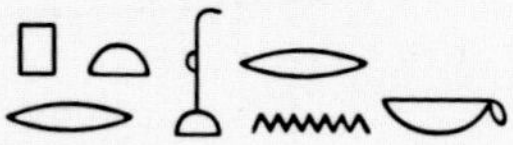

ptr rn- k
peter ren- ek
"What is your name?"

ḫrd s mꜥr
hered s meer
"Her child is happy"

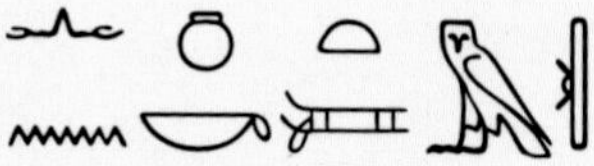

nn ink tm
nen enk tem
"I am not perfect"

s nb bṯn m pr- f
s neb betch-en em pair- ef
"Every man is disobedient in his house"

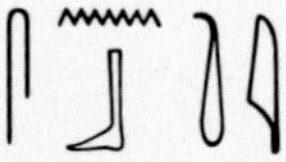

snb- ti
seneb- ti
"Goodbye"

kmt mꜥr
kemet meer
"Egypt is happy"

SOME ADDITIONAL HIEROGLYPHS

This page presents a random selection of signs that do not appear elsewhere in the book.

Around  *ḥ3*

Bald  *wš*
Be not  *tm*
Best  *stpw*
Brilliance  *i3w*

Closed  *tm*

Dig, to  *3d*

Earlier  *ḫntw*
Egg  *swḥt*
Empty  *šw*
Evening meal 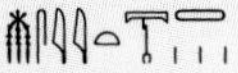 *msyt*
Explain, to  *wḥꜥw*
Eyebrows *inḥ*

However  *swt*

Is  *iw*

Jubilation  *hnw*

Later  *ḥr s3*
Lip  *spt*

Memory  *sḫ3w*
Million  *ḥḥ*

Often  *ꜥš3*

Outside of  *m ḥr s3*

Private 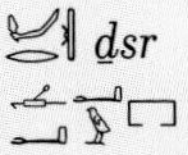 *ḏsr*
Privacy *wꜥꜥw*
Prosper, to  *rwḏ*

Rejuvenated 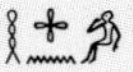 *ḥwn*

Sad  *ḏw*
Slave (male)  *ḥm*
Slave (female) *ḥm.t*
Spend all day, to  *wrš*
Spend all night, to *sḏr*
Spit, to 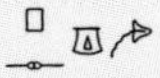 *psg*
Strength 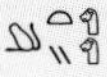 *pḥty*
Summon, to  *nis*
Sweet  *nḏm*
Sweetness  *nḏm ib*

There is/was  *iwn*
Today  *min*
Tomorrow  *m dw3(w)*
Truth 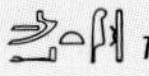 *m3ꜥt*

Unique  *wꜥty*

Walk, to  *ḫp*
Wise, to be  *s3*

Yesterday  *sf*

SIGN INDEX

This index lists all the main hieroglyphic signs that have been given as examples in the text or highlighted in marginal captions to the illustrations from tomb paintings, papyri or inscriptions. The signs are listed alphabetically by English translation. If you are using this book as a guide to recognizing and translating inscriptions at Egyptian sites or in museums, this listing provides a handy reference to help you recall hieroglyphic combinations you have encountered in the text. A full index of the book's contents follows on page 172.

A

Abomination *bwt*
Adore, to *dw3*
Advice *sḫr*
Aggressive *3d*
Agreeable *nḏm*
All *nb*
Amount *rḫt*
Amulet *s3*
Amun *ꜥimn*
Amusement *sḫmḫ-ib*
Anger *ḳnd*
Angry *ḳnd* or *ḏnd*
Anointing *sft*
Anointing oil *sft*
Another *ky*
Anubis *ꜥinpw* or *ꜥinpw*
Arm *ꜥ*
Army *mšꜥ*
Arrow *šsr*
Ascent *k3y*
As *m* or *r*
As to *r*
Attack, to *tkk*
Atum *ꜥitm*
Axe *3ḳḫw*

B

Bad *bin*
Baker *rtḥty*
Barley *it*
Be, to *wnn*
Beauties *nfrw*
Beautiful *nfr*
Beer *ḥnḳt*
Beget, to *wtt*
Bird *3pd*
Blood *snf*
Boat *dpt*
Body *ḫt*
Bowing to the ground *ksw*
Bowman *pḏty*
Bowstring *rwd*
Bread *t*
Breast *mnd*
Breath *t3w*
Breath, lack of *itmw*
Breathe, to *ssn* or *tpi*
Breeze *swt*
Bright *ḥḏ*
Brother *sn*
Build, to *ḳd*
Bulti fish *int*
Butler *wdpw*
Bury, to *ḳrs*
By *in* or *n*

C

Cartouche *mnš*
Carve, to *mnḫ*
Cat *miw*
Cattle *mnmnt* or *iḥw*
Chantress *šmꜥit*
Chapel *k3(r)i* or *r-pr*
Chariot *wrrt*
Charm, to *i3mt*
Chatter, to *ꜥš(3)-r*
Chief *wr* or *ḥ3ty-ꜥ* or *sr*
Child *ẖrd*
Children *msw*
City *niwt*
Clothes *ḥbs*

Coffin *ḳrsw*
Collar *wsḫ*
Come forth, to *prt*
Commander *ṯsw*
Commoners *rḫyt*
Conjure, to *šn* or *šnw*
Contented *ḥtp*
Copper *bi3*
Copulate, to *nk*
Courtier *smr*
Count, to *ip*
Countryside *sḫt*
Create, to *sḫpr*
Crocodile *msḥ*
Cry out, to *sbḥ*
Cubit *mḥ*
Cultivate, to *ḫbs*
Cup *ꜥꜥb*
Curse *sḥwr*

D

Dagger *b3gsw*
Dance, to *ḫb*
Daughter *s3t*
Day *rꜥ*
Deaf *sḫ*
Death *mwt*
Deben *dbn*
Delta *t3-mḥw*
Desert *dšrt*
Desire, to *mri* or *ib*
Destroy, to *ḥdi*
Diadem *nfr-ḥ3t*

Die, to *mwt*
Difficult *ḳsn* or *št3*
Disagreeable *ḳsn*
Disease *mr*
Disobedient *bṯn*
Divine *nṯrr*
Djed *ḏd*
Do, to *iri*
Do not (imperative) *m*
Doctor *swnw*
Dog *ṯsm*
Door *sb3*
Drink, to *sw(r)i*
Drive out, to *dr*
Drunken *tḫi*
Drunkenness *tḫi*
Dwell, to *ḥmsi*

E

Earth *t*
East *i3bty*
Eat, to *wnm*
Egypt (the "black land") *kmt*
Embalm, to *sdwḥ*
Embrace, to *ink*
Emmer wheat *bdt*
Enemy *ḫfty*
Envelop, to *ink*
Estate *pr-ḏt*
Eternally *ḏt* or *nḥḥ*
Eternity *nḥḥ*

Evening *mšrw*
Every *nb*
Examine, to *ḫ3*
Excellent *iḳr*
Exorcise, to *šnw*
Eye of Horus *wḏ3t*

F

Face *ḥr* or *ḫnt*
Falcon of Horus on standard *ḥr*
Falcon of Horus on sign for gold *ḥr-n nbw*
Father *it*
Festival *ḥb* or *ḥb*
Field *3ḥt*
Fight (noun) *ꜥḥ3* or *ꜥḥ3*
Fight, to *ꜥḥ3*
Find, to *gm*
Fire *ḫt*
Fish *rm*
Flame *sḏt*
Flee, to *wꜥr*
Flower *ḥrrt*
Fly, to *p3*
Food *šbw*
Foot *rd*
Foreign country *ḫ3st*
Foreigner *šm3*
Forgive, to *ḥtpn*
Fortress *mnw*
Fragrance *idt* or *idt*
Friend *ḫnms*
From *m*

Fury *ḳnd*
Furious *ḳnd* or *ḏnd*

G

Garden *ḥnt-š*
Gardener *k3ny*
Geb *gb*
Gentle *sfn*
Give, to *rdi*
Go forth, to *pri*
Go north, to *ḫdi*
Go south, to *ḫnti*
God *nṯr* or *nṯr*
Gold nbw
Good *nfr*
Goodbye snb-ti
Goose *3pd*
Granary *šnwt*
Great *wr* or *ꜥ3*
Greedy *ḥnt*

H

Hail (greeting) *hy*
Happy *mꜥr*
Hard *rwd*
Hasten, to *h3h*
He *f* or *sw*
Head *tp*
Healthy *snb*
Hear, to *sḏm*
Heart *ib*
Heaven *ḥrt*
Heket *ḥḳt*
Her *s* or *sy*
Hereditary *rpi*
Hers *s*
Him *f* or *sw*
His *f*
Hittite kingdom *ḫt*
Hoe *ḥbs*
Honey *bit*
Horizon *3ḫt*
Horus *ḥr*
House *pr*
Hunger *ḥkr*
Hunt *bḥs* or *bḥs*
Husband *h3y* or *h3y*

I

I *i* or *wi*
Ill *mr*
Image *twt*
Important *wr*
In *m*
Interior *ḫnw*
Inundation *3ḫt* or *i3ḫi*
Invoke, to *njs*
Isis *3st*
Island *iw*
It *f* or *sw* (masc.); *s* or *sy* (fem.)
Its *f* (masc.); *s* (fem.)

J

Jubilee *ḥb-sd*

K

Karnak *ꜥIpt-swt*
Khepri *ḫpri*
Khnum *ẖnmw*
King *nsw* or *n*
King of Upper and Lower Egypt *nsw-bit*
King's title (the Good God) *nṯr-nfr*
Kingship *ni-swt*
Kiss, to *sn*
Kite or Qite *ḳt*
Know, to *rḫ*
Knowing *rḫ*
Kush *k3š*

L

Lapis Lazuli *ḫsbd*
Large *wr*
Lector priest *ḫr(y)-ḥbt*
Let (expressing wish) *imi*
Libation priest *ibh*
Life *ꜥnḫ*
Listen, to *sḏm*
Live, to *ꜥnḫ*
Lord *nb* or *nb*
Lord of the two lands *nb nswt t3wy*
Lotus pool *š3*
Love, to *mri* or *mri*

M

Mace *ḥḏ*
Magic (noun) *ḥk3* or *ḥk3*
Magical utterance *r*
Magical utterances *ḥk3w*

Magistrate *ḏ3ḏ3t*
Maid *ḥm.t*
Majesty *ḥm*
Make, to *iri*
Man *s* or *s*
Mankind *rmṯ*
Manservant *b3k*
Many *ꜥš3*
Marshland *sḫt*
Mayor *ḥ3ty-ꜥ*
Me *i* or *wi*
Measure, to *ḫ3i*
Meat *wꜥbt*
Military expedition *wḏit*
Milk *irtt*
Mine (noun) *ḫ3t*
Miner *iky*
Mirror *ꜥnḫ*
Mistress *nbt*
Mistress of the house *nbt-pr*
Monkey *ky*
Month *3bd*
Monument *mnw*
More than *r*
Morning *dw3t*
Mother *mwt*
Mourning *ikb*
Mourn, to *i3kb*
Mummy *wi*
Mut *mwt*
Mutilated *i3ṯ*
My *i*

N

Name *rn*
Near *ḥr*
Necropolis *ẖr(t)-nṯr*
Noble *sr*
No *nn*
Nomad *šm3*
Nome *sp(3)t* or *sp(3)t*
North *t3-mḥw*
North, to go *ḫdi*
Nose *fnd*
Not *n* or *nn*
Nubian *mḏ3iw* or *nḥsy* or *iwnt*
Number *rḫt*
Nurse *rnn*
Nut (goddess) *nwt*

O

Obelisk *ṯḫn*
Odour *sty*
Of *n* or *m*
Offer, to *ḥnp*
Offering piles *ꜥ3bt*
Office *ḫ3*
Official *sr*
Oil *mrḥt*
Old *i3w*
On *ḥr* or *ḥr*
Osiris *wsir*
Our *n*
Overseer *imy-r*

P

Pain *3ḫw*
Palace *ꜥḥ*
Palm (measure) *ḏbꜥ*
Peace *ḥtpw*
Peasant *sḫty*
People *rmṯ*
Perfect *tm*
Phallus *ḥnn*
Pharaoh *pr-ꜥ3*
Plan *sḫr* or *sḫr*
Pleasure *sḫmḫ-ib*
Pleasure, to take *ḫntš*
Plough, to *sk3*
Poor man *nḏs*
Praise (noun) *i3w* or *ḥnw*
Pray, to *nḥi*
Precious stones *ꜥ3t*
Pregnant, to become *iwr*
Priest *wꜥb*
Priest, serving in temple *wnwt*
Priesthood *wnwt*
Prince, hereditary *ḥ3ty-ꜥ*
Ptah *ptḥ*
Pyramid *mr*
Pyramid tomb *mr*

Q

Quarry (mine) *ḫ3t*

R

Rain storm *snm(w)*
Re *rꜥ*
Reap, to *3sḫ* or *3sḫ*
Recite, to *ḏd*
Recreation *sḫmḫ-ib*
Red Crown *dšrt*
Red Land *dšrt*

Remedy *pẖrt*
Rest, to *ḥtpn*
Rise, to *wbn*
River *itrw*
River-measure *itrw*
Rod *ḫt*
Rot, to *ḥw3*
Rule, to *ḥḳ3*

S

Sacred *wꜥb*
Saw *m33*
Say, to *ḏd-mdw*
Scribe *sš*
Sculpt, to *ḫti*
Sculptor *gnwty*
Sea *w3ḏ-wr*
Season *tr* or *tr*
Season of inundation *3ḫt*
Sed festival *ḥb-sd*
Servant *ḥry-pr*
Seth *s(w)tḫ* or *s(w)tḫ*
Shadow *šwt*
She *s* or *sy*
Shield *ikm*
Shoot *st*
Sickle *m3*
Signet ring *ḏbꜥt*
Silver *ḥḏ*
Singer *šmꜥit*
Sister *snt*
Skipper *nfw*
Sky *pt*
Sleep, to *ꜥwy*
Small boy *šri*
Smite, to *sḳr*
Snake *ḥf3w* or *ḥf3w*
Snare, to (birds) *sḫt*
Sobek *sbk*
Soldier *wꜥw*
Soldiers *mnfyt*
Son *s3*
South *rśwt*
South, to go *ḫnti*
Southerners *rsiw*
Sovereign *iti*
Spew out, to *ḳ3ꜥ*
Spirit *k3*
Staff *mdw*
Statue, Resemblance *twt*
Stone *jnr*
Suckle, to *snḳ*
Summer *šmw*
Sun *rꜥ* or *rꜥ*
Sweet *nḏm*
Sword *sft*
Syria *rṯnw*

T

Table of offerings *ḫ3w(t)*
Taste, to *dp*
Temple *ḥwt-nṯr* or *ḥwt-ꜥ3t*
Terror *nri*
Thebes *w3st*
Their *sn*
Them *sn*
There! *iḫ*
They *sn*
Things *ḫt*
Thirst *ib*
Thirsty, to be *ibi*
Thoth *ḏḥwty*
Through (out of) *in*
Throwstick *ꜥmꜥ3t*
Time *rk*
To *r*
To (a person) *n*
Together with *ḥnꜥ*
Tomb *3ḫt*
Tomb chamber *is*
Tooth *ibḥ*
Toward *r*
Treasury *pr-ḥḏ*
Tribute *inw*
Turquoise *mfk3t*

U

Under *ḫr*
Under (the rule of) *ḫr*
Underworld *d(w)3t*
Unit commander *ṯsw*
Upper Egypt *šmꜥw*
Upon *ḥr*
Us *n*

V

Victory *nḫtw*
Vigorous *rwd*
Vizier *ṯ3ty*
Voice *ḫrw*

W

War cry *hmhmt*
Warrior *ꜥḥ3* or *ꜥḥ3*

Washerman *rḫty*
Water *mw*
We *n*
We two *ny*
Weep, to *rmi*
West *imnt*
Wet nurse *mnꜥ*
What *ptr*
Why *ḥr m*
Widow *ẖ3rt* or *ẖ3rt*
Wife *ḥmt* or *nbt-pr*

Wine *irp*
Winter *prt*
Wish, to *mrr*
With *m*
Woman *ḥmt* or *st* or *nbt-pr*
Work *b3k*
Worry, to *snḏ*
Worship, to *sns*
Wrathful, to be *ḏnd*
Write, to *sš*
Wring, to (bird's neck) *wšn*

Y

Year *rnpt* or *rnpt*
Yes *tw*
You *k* or *ṯw* (masc. sing.); *ṯ* or *ṯn* (fem. sing.); *ṯn*, (pl.)
You two *ṯny*
Young, to be *ḥwn*
Your *k* (masc. sing.); *ṯ* (fem. sing.); *ṯn*, (pl.)
Youthful *rnpi*

BIBLIOGRAPHY AND FURTHER READING

Adkins, L. and Adkins, R. *The Keys of Egypt*, HarperCollins, 2000

Allen, J. P. *Middle Egyptian: An Introduction to the Language and Culture of Hieroglyphs*, Cambridge University Press, 2000

Breasted, J. H. *Ancient Records of Egypt*, Vols I–V, University of Illinois Press, 2001

Faulkner, R. O. *A Concise Dictionary of Middle Egyptian*, Aris and Phillips, 1962

Fischer, H. G. *Ancient Egyptian Calligraphy: A Beginner's Guide to Writing Hieroglyphs*, Metropolitan Museum of Art, 1998

Forman, W. and Quirke, S. *Hieroglyphs and the Afterlife in Ancient Egypt*, British Museum Press, 1996

Gardiner, A. *Egyptian Grammar*, Aris and Phillips, 1957

Lichtheim, M. *Ancient Egyptian Literature*, Vols. I and II, University of California Press, 1975

Malek, J. *The ABC of Hieroglyphics*, Ashmolean Museum Publications, 1994

Moran, W. L. *The Amarna Letters*, The Johns Hopkins University Press, 1992

Parkinson, R. B. *Cracking Codes: The Rosetta Stone*, British Museum Press, 1999

Parkinson, R. B. *Voices From Ancient Egypt: An Anthology of Middle Kingdom Writings*, British Museum Press, 1991

Walters, C. C. *An Elementary Coptic Grammar of the Sahidic Dialect*, Aris and Phillips, 1977

Watterson, B. *Introducing Egyptian Hieroglyphs*, 2nd edition, Scottish Academic Press, 1993

Watterson, B. *More About Egyptian Hieroglyphs*, Scottish Academic Press, 1986

INDEX

NOTE: Page numbers in italic refer to captions.

ACKNOWLEDGMENTS

The publisher would like to thank Helen Strudwick for her assistance with the hieroglyphs. The publisher would also like to thank the people, museums and photographic libraries listed below for permission to reproduce their material. Every care has been taken to trace copyright holders. However, if we have omitted anyone we apologize and will, if informed, make corrections in any future edition. We have used the following abbreviations.

BM: The British Museum

JL: Jürgen Liepe/The Egyptian Museum, Cairo, Egypt

Page 1 BM (EA117); **3** BM (EA99013); **4** BM (EA24); **5** BM (EA10471/21); **7** Art Archive/Cairo Museum/Dagli Orti; **8–9** BM (EA10470/6); **11** BM (EA24); **14** AKG/Louvre; **17** JL/ Cairo Museum (JE38368=CG42127); **18** JL (JE54313); **21** AKG/ Erich Lessing; **23** BM (EA64661); **25** Art Archive; **26–7** Art Archive/Cairo Museum/Dagli Orti; **28–9** AKG/Erich Lessing; **31** Bridgeman Art Library/BM; **32** AKG/Kunsthistorisches Museum, Vienna; **34–5** JL (JE46724=CG76); **37** Corbis/Roger Wood; **39** Bridgeman Art Library; **41** BM (EA10470/33); **42** AKG/Cairo Museum; **44** AKG/Henning Bock; **46–7** BM (EA10471/21); **48–9** Graham Harrison; **51** AKG/Erich Lessing; **52** AKG/Erich Lessing; **53** JL (JE48035); **55** BM (EA22332); **56** BM (EA37984); **58–9** Art Archive/Louvre/Dagli Orti; **61** BM (EA999/24); **62** Robert Harding Picture Library, London; **65** JL (CG48406); **67** AKG/Louvre; **68** Corbis/Dagli Orti; **71** Werner Forman Archive, London; **73** JL (JE42948); **74–5** JL (SR11488); **77** JL (CG3&CG4); **78–9** BM (EA3077); **80** JL (JE4673=CG52645); **81** JL (61467); **83** BM (EA117); **84** The Stock Market, London; **87** AKG/Museo Archaeologico, Florence; **88** BM (EA99013); **91** Stone/Getty One; **92–3** Art Archive/Devizes Museum/ Eileen Tweedy; **95** AKG/Rijksmuseum van Oudheden, Leiden; **97** BM (EA10686); **99** AKG/Kunsthistorisches Museum, Vienna; **101** BM (EA41549); **102–103** Robert Harding Picture Library, London; **105** AKG/Erich Lessing; **105** BM (K69842); **106** JL (JE44866); **109** AKG/Kunsthistorisches Museum, Vienna; **110** BM (EA198144); **112–13** JL (JE15210=CG394); **114** JL (JE32018=CG257); **116-17** JL (JE10065=CG20); **119** AKG/Erich Lessing; **121** Bridgeman Art Library/Fitzwilliam Museum, Cambridge; **123** JL (JE30986); **125** Art Archive/Cairo Museum/Dagli Orti; **127** Art Archive/Dagli Orti; **128** JL (JE40679); **130** BM (EA10470/30); **132–3** Chris Caldicott; **134** Art Archive/Dagli Orti; **136–7** Art Archive/Cairo Museum/ Dagli Orti; **139** Corbis/Artur Yann-Bertrand; **140** AKG/Erich Lessing; **143** Art Archive/BM; **144** BM (EA10554/81); **147** JL (JE72171); **149** Bridgeman Art Library/Giraudon; **150–51** AKG/ Erich Lessing